Stellar Management Teams

Management teams at all levels, and individual team members in particular, are often disengaged and disconnected from the management function itself. Statements such as, „we lack common goals or they are unclear‰„I have no influence‰,I am not listened to nor taken into account‰and „I do not feel valued – actually, nobody does‰are commonplace. The authors argue this is because we have been entrenched in an era of guru leadership but that it must come to an end if our management teams are to rise to the top. An individual is not capable of controlling the complicated system of an organization, with its countless variables, especially in conjunction with the rapid change in both the economy and market forces, which are unpredictable and uncontrollable. No matter how talented the individual, no one person is in a position to manage this complex system alone – not even a guru leader.

The authors contend that what is needed now are resilient trendsetters who will bring about a new era of top-performing teams that together form a „collective guru‰which they refer to as a Stellar Management Team.

In this book, the reader undertakes a metaphorical journey to the stars, which symbolizes top-level interaction and collaboration. The journey is the development from an ordinary management team into a Stellar Management Team, which elevates its operation up to a new level of performance and success.

Vesa Ristikangas is a Senior Leadership Coach and Partner at BoMentis, a business and management consultancy in Finland.

Tapani Rinne is a Trainer, Personal Resilience Coach, and CEO and founder of Ambitio Group, Finland.

Stellar Management Teams

Vesa Ristikangas and Tapani Rinne

Routledge
Taylor & Francis Group

LONDON AND NEW YORK

First published 2018
by Routledge
2 Park Square, Milton Park, Abingdon, Oxon OX14 4RN

and by Routledge
711 Third Avenue, New York, NY 10017

Routledge is an imprint of the Taylor & Francis Group, an informa business

© 2018 Vesa Ristikangas and Tapani Rinne

British Library Cataloguing-in-Publication Data
A catalogue record for this book is available from the British Library

Library of Congress Cataloging-in-Publication Data
Names: Ristikangas, Vesa, 1971– author. | Rinne, Tapani, 1955– author.
Title: Stellar management teams / Vesa Ristikangas and Tapani Rinne.
Description: Abingdon, Oxon ; New York, NY : Routledge, 2018. | Includes
     bibliographical references and index.
Identifiers: LCCN 2017038826 (print) | LCCN 2017047320 (ebook) |
     ISBN 9781351244114 (eBook) | ISBN 9780815372943 (hardback :
     alk. paper) | ISBN 9780815373131 (pbk. : alk. paper)
Subjects: LCSH: Management. | Teams in the workplace. | Leadership.
Classification: LCC HD31.2 (ebook) | LCC HD31.2 .R57 2018 (print) |
     DDC 658.4/022· dc23
LC record available at https://lccn.loc.gov/2017038826

ISBN: 978-0-8153-7294-3 (hbk)
ISBN: 978-0-8153-7313-1 (pbk)
ISBN: 978-1-351-24411-4 (ebk)

Typeset in Times New Roman
by Apex CoVantage, LLC

Contents

Figures

Tables

WAKE UP!

Throughout the ages, we have placed on a pedestal those business leaders and warlords who have achieved victories and breakthroughs. They are charismatic, guru-class individuals, mostly men, who are worshipped and glorified. They are heroes of best-seller biographies, and their stories make readers believe in individualistic excellence. This book is an exception. Here you will not find praise of star leaders nor exaltation of individual heroism. The reason is obvious. An individual is NOT capable of controlling the complicated system of an organization, with its countless variables in simultaneous motion. Rapid changes both in the economic structure of the world and in market forces with their surprising influence in every business are totally uncontrollable. No matter how talented the individual, no one is in a position to manage this complex system alone – not even a guru leader.

Wake up! Why do we need a book about a Stellar Team?

Today, a director needs all the wisdom from across the organization and all available human resources, in order to be able to cope with all the challenges of the future. Instead of guru leadership the organizations need more community spirit and actions that will motivate a change from individual fighting to team play. Now we need strong trendsetters to start a new era of excellent management teams, that together form a „collective guru‰ which we call a Stellar Team. There is a need for a new way of thinking and acting, new structures and policies that help the Stellar Team to guarantee the true success of their organization. We are talking about a team that knows how to play together seamlessly and how to reach its common goal.

Wake up! What is going on in management teams?

During the past years, we have repeatedly heard from management teams at many levels and from individual intelligent members some very strange statements:

- Our management team lacks common goals, or at least, they are unclear.
- Our management team is, in reality, a pack of lone wolves running around.
- I have no influence in the management team, I am not listened to nor taken into account.

- The participation of other members is a sham, our management team has free riders.
- The interaction among the members of our management team is very weak; no questions, no listening, no conversation – and silence when it comes to obvious issues.
- I do not feel valued – actually, nobody does.
- The management team members play solo outside the team, they do not hold to joint decisions.
- Our management team makes no decisions, or at least the implementation of decisions is lame, we do not achieve what is agreed.

Is it worth going on with that kind of theatre called Management Team? Is it worth jogging along the same old runway, if there is a possibility to change style, to accelerate and to take off?

Wake up! Is there something wrong with management teams?

Many of our readers represent healthy, well-functioning management teams, whose ambitious goal is to move from good to excellent. That is a great goal. This book will surely be a support for this aim of constant improvement. However, the improvement is most needed in management teams who think they are functioning „normally‰they imagine they are collaborating and they believe that they are achieving the best possible result.

We think the biggest nuisance in management teams is *hypohealth*. This causes thoughtlessness, which, in turn, feeds so-called management team diseases, that erode the results of the whole organization. These erosive diseases are invisible, but their effects are often very visible and tangible.

No one wants to cause diseases intentionally, because they prevent cooperation and considerable energy is wasted. The management team detects painful symptoms, but the pain is tolerated with gritted teeth. If the suffering is treated, the only method is to use medication that numbs the pain without making any attempts to detect or remove the disease pathogens.

This book offers a completely new approach to management team diseases. It applies broad-spectrum antibiotics and provides a cure for management teams. The book acts as a self-help guide for collaboration and also in the creation of a healthy management team.

Wake up! Is this going to be just another -ism or some soft leadership mumbo jumbo?

We know that management team diseases are treatable. Our knowledge is based on research and on our own experiences of leadership teams, that have wanted to be cured. As the management team begins to find sufficient collective will, even the worst diseases will disappear. Those who seek to coach Stellar Teams are guided by the following principles of coaching and care:

- Individuals need each other to grow and to benefit from their potential.
- The potential in a management team can be harnessed, if there is a will to do so.
- There is no single trick or technique that makes a Stellar Team, but there is a need for an ability to see specific characteristics and the logic of your thinking system.
- The majority of factors for real change remain concealed if the attention of the management team is directed only towards measurable parameters.
- The Stellar Team needs coaching leadership, which is based on appreciative, all-inclusive and target-oriented action.
- If you want to travel fast, go alone, if you want to travel far, go together.

So, you think you are awake? Be part of our joint journey then!

Management team diseases must definitely be treated, if the management team aims at attaining stellar level. Stellar Team, Guiding Star and Journey are this book̂s metaphors for collaboration within a top team, and for quality focus and top-class results. We have divided the book into four parts.

PART I – We assume that your management team wants to be a Stellar Team, which is going to take off on a journey to the stars. To make this possible you have to become aware of gravity factors that keep you in your routine operations. Carelessness forms a ubiquitous gravity that you must overcome in order to be able to take off. In particular, we shall provoke new thinking with systemic thinking perspectives. We will present our guiding star model, which is based on our experience and on research into team effectiveness. It is a model in which both Primary and Secondary Goals guide the management team in developing their collaboration to a new level.

PART II – Here we will start to build a strong launch pad for our journey to the stars. We shall look at the Secondary Goals of a management team, which constitute the attention focus for activities and a framework for common success. Once your management team knows what you are doing and why, you are already well advanced. Mutual practices in the team add further strength to the launch pad. They also ensure the efficiency of your mutual time management and the consideration of relevant stakeholders in decision-making.

PART III – We will concentrate on the attraction or the gravity of the star, which really makes the Stellar Team commit to development. We look at the Primary Goals of management team, which are the factors that make your management teamŝ engine obtain its optimal performance. We will direct your attention onto how the management team operates as a team, and on how it can be more than the sum of its parts. On your journey to the stars you need to focus on Primary

Goals, i.e., inter alia, the conscious use of diversity in your team, building an open feedback culture and strengthening mutual trust in your team.

PART IV – We will bring more perspectives onto how the Stellar Team will keep to the direction given of their chosen guiding star. You will need leadership, which brings the best out of each team member. If the members of your management team are able to take on different roles flexibly and adjust their behaviour, they will likely avoid getting stuck. You will be able to take advantage of group energy. On the way to the stars your management team will come to many bends and obstacles that will make your common journey more difficult. The real Stellar Team will not get confused by the bends, but will be able to return quickly to the right path.

Waking up – what are the impacts?

Reading this book will give you a clear understanding of how your management will take the development journey to becoming a Stellar Team. Finding a cure for many diseases will most certainly attract you but taking off on that journey will not be easy. Development means always abandoning the old – and it is a giant step into the new and unknown.

WAKE UP! IF YOU WANT TO IMPROVE AND ACHIEVE MORE, YOU HAVE TO START YOUR JOURNEY. – COWARDS, YOU'D BETTER MOVE YOURSELVES, TOO.

If collaboration in your management team were simple and easy, you wouldn't be reading this book. If developing collaboration was only difficult, we would not have written anything about it.

Vesa & Tapani

Acknowledgements

First we want to thank a few top professionals for their concrete support. In our background interviews we gained valuable perspectives from experienced management team members like Juha Harju and Jussi Tolvanen. We received great assistance from directors, who read the first version of our book and gave us excellent suggestions on how to improve its contents. Our sincere thanks go to Eija Holmström, Ilkka Hallavo, Kari Paananen, Katri Sipilä, Matti Vanhanen, Matti Ylilammi, Mikael Jungner ja Pekka Pättiniemi. Furthermore we would like to give a special thank you to our numerous *incognito* helpers.

Second, we would like to thank all the management team members, directors and other participants in our trainings, who have taught us over the years. Thank you for all the challenges, feedback, success and inspiration. It is thanks to them, that we continued and that we are now here with this book.

Third, all of our back-up forces deserve a big thank you. The most important certainly are all BoMentis-colleagues: Marjut Hallavo, Marjo-Riitta Ristikangas, Antti Soikkanen, Jukka Sundberg, Hedy Kapri and Leni Grünbaum. Tapanis additional special thanks go still to Leena Rinne, also in this project, a personal supporter above all the others.

Gratefully
Vesa & Tapani

P.S. This could be taken for granted, but good cooperation does not just come automatically, not even among the top guys. We believe there cannot be too much positive feedback, and therefore one more expression of gratitude: Vesa thanks Tapani and Tapani thanks Vesa. Star duos collaboration on this book was productive, inspiring, progressive, smooth, functioning, intellectually challenging, broadening, expeditious, rewarding, efficient and – wake up: simply fantastic! The conquest of the stars continues . . .

Part I

Do you want to fly?

Figure PI.1 Star

1 Not thinking is heavy

On this planet there are countless management teams, and at many organizational levels. They remain with their feet firmly on the ground, focusing strictly on the playing field, their backpacks filled with the realities of everyday life. Still, many management teams produce incredibly hollow speeches, and if you look at the results of their words and deeds, they do not get much air under their wings. You might even wonder to what extent you would hold up your management team as an example to your own organization. A critical thinker might respond: not least regarding the quality of thinking. Thinking is like the old law of gravity in physics that we learn at schools on our planet, and that's what we can't surmount.

Provoke thinking with gravity factors

The journey to the stars starts with a new way of thinking. Many management teams act without deeper thinking. Conventional practices rule and things are handled in meetings in a routine manner. After all, they are representatives of management; they should be acting in an adult manner, playing on the same playground and cooperating well. Many members of management teams are at the top of their careers. They are compelling, they are leading experts and top influencers in their own field. They hold regular meetings and aim at wise decisions – trying to act as flag-bearers of the organization and showing the way for all. Business as usual.

Success requires that the management team begins to grow as a team. Thinking that will lead to actual results is generated through three clear questions:

- How does this team cooperate and use its common time?
- How does this team take advantage of experience and know-how that is available in the team?
- How does this team direct its time, cooperation and know-how towards a common goal?

Top talents do not automatically form a united, functional team that progresses towards a common goal through mutual support. The common benefit is easily forgotten, and individuals easily start to fiercely protect their own territories. Productivity objectives charge activities with a permanent background tension.

> *A representative of middle management told us: My supervisor is really busy all the time. The best way to catch him is to send him messages during the management team meeting. I´ve noticed that he´s then available for me and responds actively to his emails.*

Management team members can have a very quick way of functioning. Despite the speed, the force of gravity has a firm hold on them and the level of results does not display any real signs of taking off. The phenomenon described as „flying low%´is not real flying. The following is a list of ordinary gravitational factors, which prevent the speed of management team from becoming a real take off.

Gravity Factor No. 1: Emphasizing individual responsibility

It is quite natural in a management team that for each issue on the meeting agenda there will be a person responsible. So far so good; this simplifies meeting practices significantly. However, individual responsibilities get in the way of strengthening collective responsibility. A true culture of cooperation cannot emerge in a management team unless the main task is shared.

Gravity Factor No. 2: Multitude of bilateral discussions

It is typical for a management team meeting that the discussion goes between the chair and the person responsible for the issue. If these bilateral discussions start to dominate the meeting, collective responsibility vanishes. At worst, the management team will be a place where everyone knows that they are only responsible for their individual, dedicated topics. Then everyone is allocated a certain amount of time and has a well-prepared monologue in his or her laptop. As the listeners are just thinking about their own responsibilities, they will hardly ask any questions. Their attention is perhaps on fine-tuning their own monologues. The manager acting as chairman of the meeting is the only one commenting on the presentations.

Gravity Factor No. 3: Dominance of numeric indicators

Management teams have profit and loss responsibility, so controlling figures is an important part of meetings. However, if the aspired outcomes are defined only through increased revenue or reduced cost structure, there is no space for collective responsibility. Why not? Management by Numbers emphasizes the outcome and consequences of the operations. The management team misses the opportunity to flexibly determine where its members want to bring their collective responsibility to bear. Mere figures do not generate commitment. The attention is directed too much into the rear view mirror and not on activities that will ensure better figures for tomorrow. In addition, the numeric management team misses out on indicators that are based on qualitative criteria.

Gravity Factor No. 4: Tight schedules and overloaded agendas

Management team meetings are an important forum for collective decision-making. However, the meetings are run through rapidly, item by item, keeping to the agreed schedule. In that haste, the essential is forgotten: open conversation and exchange of views, as well as solving problems together. Unfortunately, no strengthening of solidarity can be accommodated within those long agendas and tight schedules.

Gravity Factor No. 5: Fixed roles

Management team members typically have quite specific job descriptions. There are roles like HR Director, Financial Director, Sales Director, IT Director etc. The responsibilities are defined, and, so far so good – life is much more clarified. At the same time, however, individuals who adhere too strictly to their roles, prevent the development of collective responsibility. Typically, members of the management team do not dare, or do not want to step on the toes of a colleague by taking a position on mutual issues. And if mutual issues do not even exist, it is appropriate to restrict the unique skills and personality of each member so that these are utilised only in their own private boxes. Long live titles and letĥs conceal knowledge in silos!

Gravity Factor No. 6: Director-centricity prevents taking responsibility

The key task of a management team is decision-making. On the other hand, management teams operate very much in a culture, in which only the CEO is responsible for the decisions taken. This is in most cases also a legal fact. Consequently, you can hear often that management teams are just pawns to be used for the CEOĥs purposes. The pawns shun responsibility, they fear opportunities and cower behind the back of the CEO. In particular, concealing liability can be very attractive in situations where you must make hard decisions. When they move into non-decision-maker mode, the team limits its learning opportunities:

• to expand and optimize their available leadership skills
• to develop the personal decision-making skills of each individual
• to experience bearing the responsibility for the decision.

Gravity Factor No. 7: The loud ones override the quiet

A management team is a group of personalities and the differences become visible in daily operations. There are always two or three members who take the centre stage and dominate the collective discussion. As these „loud ones% take more space the „quiet ones% retreat even more. If no action is taken, the natural styles of individuals take over, and at the same time the possibilities for a broader responsibility are reduced. It would take a fair amount of new thinking, to make some people exercise interest in other peopleĥs ideas, and for some others respectively to exercise being more courageous in putting forward their own ideas.

Observations in a management team meeting in a technology company:

• *Everyone had a laptop computer on the table, everyone was bustling about with their own activities.*
• *The meeting was almost entirely a monologue by the CEO.*

- *There were hardly any questions, management team members were mainly silent or hummed quietly.*
- *A common objective was impossible to detect, because the issues were so specific, independent of each other, and seemed to be very trivial.*
- *Several members left in the middle of the meeting, of course politely apologizing, but without any justification – something else was in any case more important than the management team meeting.*

Slow thinking combined with fast decisions

It is said that mistakes are made in thoughtlessness. On the other hand people are certainly thinking in management teams, all brain activity is rarely completely absent. However, activities will continue endlessly on the same track, unless the team wakes up to think about how it thinks.

Here we get great support from Daniel Kahneman, an Israeli-American psychologist and researcher. He was awarded the Nobel Memorial Prize in Economic Sciences in 2002 for his work on behavioural economics. Kahneman has examined, in particular, the process of evaluation and decision-making models. As a basis for the improvement of thinking we borrow Daniel Kahneman's simplified idea, according to which thinking happens in our brains in two alternative systems.

System 1: fast, instinctive and emotional

Illustrative expressions: automatic and autonomous, effortless and fast, no need for working memory, connected to stimuli, originates from early human evolution. An important caution: ease of thought generation gives an illusion of truth. In this book, we call this way of thinking simply *Hasty Intuition.*

System 2: slow, more careful and more logical

Descriptive terms: conscious, slow, voluntary, requires working memory, analytical, abstraction, what-if imagination, evaluation, options, reflective, originates from later evolution, specific for human species. In this book, we term this way of thinking *Deep Analysis.*

The management team is, even in its wisdom, still very lazy when it comes to using brains. In addition the modern world demands quick solutions. Therefore we mostly use System 1, i.e. Hasty Intuition is in charge and we let the analytical Deep Analysis take a rest.

Hasty Intuition takes us fast – even astray

Rational decision-making requires the skill to stop and to question the answer produced by Hasty Intuition. On the other hand, daily life would be really difficult if every choice had to be analysed. Intuitive decision-making has overcome in human evolution, because it has provided the correct answer enough times – and that answer has come immediately. In other words, Hasty Intuition, as well as Deep Analysis, are both important for smooth-running daily life.

Intuition, which is „the information that we are not aware of‰seems to appear today, more and more often, even from management as a major justification for decisions. Hasty Intuition (System 1) has its advantages but also its defects and biases. Its intuitive impressions guide our thinking and behaviour very broadly – and all too often wrongly. The following are some examples of thinking biases, which may in management team situations even affect strategies within major businesses.

- The team displays excessive confidence and tolerates excessive risk taking (Hasty Intuition produces the conclusion: this idea must be correct, because even other people think so)
- Cognitive ease, i.e. the solution comes easily (Hasty Intuition produces the conclusion: the idea must be correct, because it feels familiar, real, good or kind of natural)
- Replacing difficult questions with easy ones, that is, if we do not know how to answer the question of how currency X will develop, we say that X has been strong against the Euro for a quite long time (Hasty Intuition produces an easier but logical question, and then we start happily nodding to our answer)
- The bias of the end result, i.e. because the result is good, the product must be good and vice versa, (Hasty Intuition says: this idea must be correct, as it is so logical – and, using Deep Analysis to analyse the causal relationship would be too laborious).

As we understand how these two thinking systems – especially Hasty Intuition – affect our evaluations and decisions, we can justify creating better discussions and making more-informed decisions in the management team.

Math question – A bat and a ball

This old math problem is told in Daniel KahnemanŝB book. Reply to this question first quickly, that is, let Hasty Intuition produce an answer. Then read the question again and let Deep Analysis take its time and calculate the answer.

– A bat and a ball cost a total of €110. The bat costs €100 more than the ball. How much does the ball cost?

Did you try them both? Most likely, you got two different answers, of which only the latter was correct. Intuitive thinking is worth a try, but it is better not to always rely on it as the sole way of thinking. (We tell the busy reader here that €10 from Hasty Intuition is definitely wrong.)

New thinking instead of being in a rut

In this developing world, new ideas are inevitably needed. Old ways of thinking help us only to see in the same way as before, to act as before, and to obtain the same results as before. However, developing new thinking does not start with the command „letﬁ think different now‰ Thinking reform is confronted by some general, impeding factors that we will happily use to support our old thinking. Paraphrasing the Finnish philosopher Esa Saarinen, they are crystallized in the following factors:

1.   Pride of the owner – I have ideas, they are mine and I am used to them.
2.   Sprout of dogmatism – I believe that truths are already defined, and I am not supposed to suspect them.
3.   Naïve realism – I think my own thoughts describe correctly how things are; my thoughts are not interpretations but just facts.
4.   Credulity – I believe what the others believe, or at least seem to believe.
5.   Light motives – I am not able to resist my old thoughts, especially if they are related to my enthusiasm.

In practice, the processing capacity of the brain has no connection with the renewal of thinking, but more critical is the courage to test new ways of thinking. In practice, the new thinking enables us to see things and situations in a new way. Seeing in a new way, in turn, allows us to act differently and operate in a new way. These, in turn, will be followed by new experiences and new results. Thus, the reform of thinking leads to seeing, acting and to results.

What kind of a development leap could be brought about in a management team by the development of thinking? Do we want better decisions or more decisions? How much could thinking be accelerated, without reducing decisions to wild guesses? In most cases, people say that, above all, the quality of decisions should be improved. Some guru has claimed that management teams can easily achieve this by not making poor decisions anymore.

Stop and think together

The common thinking of the management team can develop in at least two ways. First of all, by thinking of how you think, and by becoming aware of your own quick truths. The reliability of the truths can be improved by collecting more information, studying and observing. High-quality thinking cannot be just seemingly logical ideas produced by Hasty Intuition and based on a strikingly minimal amount of information.

The second way of developing your thinking is harder than the first one: slowing down. This means literally slowing down. In practice, even stopping. Stopping to think with Deep Analysis. Stopping personally and stopping together in the management team. The question is, of course, how much do we have time for thinking about the current issue.

Hasty Intuition probably says that both of these ways of developing your thinking may be impossible. But fortunately, you are at least able to stop to read this book. This could be a key step to overcome the gravity of everyday life and to lift your entire management team onto a new trajectory.

2 Systems thinking – basis of new thinking

Renewal of thinking requires more than just thinking; the management team needs new elements and new types of information as its basis. *The truth is out there*, announced an ancient TV series, referring to all-knowing aliens in outer space. But there is no use in searching for an all-knowing truth in management team thinking, not even in the stars. Suppose, however, that we need to begin the thinking by asking **what** we do know – for example, „truths%– so that we can think of **how** we know. This „how-knowing%means thinking about the relationships between things. It is the identification of the systems formed by things.

For example, if the organization is described as a system or a network of thoughts and ideas, is the management team within that network a hub or a dead weight which is better avoided? What are the relationships between the thinkers in the organization? What kinds of systems do they form? Is there a separate network of actual influencers and a system that we may call an organization chart theatre?

Requirements for management have changed in many ways. Organizations are connected in internal and external networks, their operations are information-intensive and expert-centred, the operating environments are more complex and the complexity of change has intensified. At the same time, production, technology development and management processes are linked, so that the quantity of different and various forms of relations have become unmanageable. In addition, all the operations have moved to networking, virtual and real-time, and everything is dominated by requirements of effective performance. Management teams need an understanding of broader entities, which we call systems.

New elements from systems thinking

Systemic theories and systems thinking provide a frame of reference for new management thinking. Systems theory combines perspectives from several sciences, and these perspectives all have a common feature in that they seek to understand as a wholeness. Systems thinking is therefore a holistic science for seeing systems as a wholeness. It is a frame of reference that focuses not on issues and static moments but rather on interaction, relationships and observing change models.

Systems researchers have made interesting observations on the dynamics of changes. The butterfly effect is a well-known metaphor in systems thinking, where attention is drawn to the cause-and-effect relationship. It is said that a butterfly's wing beat in Beijing may start a chain that causes a tropical storm in the Gulf of Mexico. Of course the butterfly is not changing the climate, but, however, it initiates a minute change. This change causes a new reaction, and so on, until finally the reaction chain culminates in the Gulf of Mexico.

Taking advantage of small changes creates a positive climate for change. We can process the butterfly effect for management teams and managers in simple ideas:

- Make small experiments and take initiatives, then together wonder fascinatedly about the results – and use the results in selecting your next step.
- Transfer the attention from power to influencing.
- Abandon the illusion of control and give an opportunity to set chains of positive change in motion.

The systems dictatorship

An organization, i.e. a system consisting of people, operates in a dynamic state and it renews itself continuously. A social system consists of experiences of many people, and it definitely differs from physical or chemical systems. For renewal and development the social system must keep its movement active. At the same time, it is important to find a purpose and the sense of control, and on the other hand, enough space for free thinking. At the same, we need time limits and spaciousness, because the human mind does not seem to tolerate total boundlessness and, on the other hand, too strict limits stifle creativity and prosperity. Excessive order in the system unilaterally supports dependence, which leads to immature behaviour.

Fears limit enthusiasm in a very effective way. Invisible parts of an organizational system can give birth to a mechanism that will shackle creativity, productivity and freedom. This comes to dominate the interaction so strongly that it can be called, according to Esa Saarinen, Systems Dictatorship. Based on its construction and birth mechanism we can consider Systems Dictatorship also as an organizational culture that paralyzes and impoverishes the interactions.

The key features of Systems Dictatorship are its invisibility and multi-layered nature. As with organizational culture Systems Dictatorship is formed as a result of activities over a longer period of time. From the individual's point of view it is analogous to a permanent power structure, which you are unable to affect. Within the Systems Dictatorship, one may even imagine that such a corporate culture is the only possible reality.

The driving force of the Systems Dictatorship is fear. In practice, instead of emphasizing the success of the whole entity, the individual's performance is underlined, which, in turn, nourishes the power struggle. There are also other emotions in the background highlighting the power struggle or individual responsibility. The emphasis on individual responsibility is likely to give rise to fear and envy. Individual responsibility can easily lead to malicious partial optimization.

An invisible system often hides things that people do not even want to face. As we learn to deal with these, however, we eliminate fears and other negative emotions, which prevent the emergence of good results. Productivity and efficiency will not be generated from fear but from enthusiasm.

The management team of an industrial enterprise was in a workshop analysing basic fears that may affect them in an invisible system. The team came up with a terrifying list:

- *I am not professionally credible, I don't have enough competence.*
- *I have lost my position and my grip on the job.*
- *I do not perform well enough or the quality of my work is not good enough.*
- *I am not intelligent or quick-witted enough.*
- *My ignorance is revealed as is my tendency to be emotional.*
- *I am not appreciated, not valued, not respected.*
- *My best years have already gone and there is no future for me.*
- *I am considered childish and people laugh at me.*
- *People team up against me and I am ignored.*

As the management team had the courage to make a range of fears visible, their influence began to subside. Instead of fear, trust began slowly growing in the team.

DO YOU DARE: Handle your fears

Make an experiment. Tell yourself what you are afraid of (and tell it to the rest of the management team, too, if you dare). Describe how you would act, if you did not have those fears. Now analyse your present action compared to the previous description: what similarities do you find, at least sometimes or to some degree? Write down, how you are going to increase those activities.

Eight systemic ideas for stellar team designers

Systems thinking is an important frame of reference. A short recap: systems thinking aims to see entities as a whole where the components are in a relationship and interact with each other. Systems thinking focuses on interaction between the components and observes the change models.

Even though the systemic theories sometimes stray perhaps too far from the everyday reality of organizations and management teams, systems thinking is applicable to the daily life of management teams in many ways. The higher you are in the hierarchy of your organization, the more important it is to understand complex operations and change potential in your organization. As the management team starts to see its operations and the organization as a living system, this change of mind-set will also affect other activities. Next we are going to present a collection of the most important application areas of systems thinking for the development of management teams.

Systemic Idea 1: There are invisible forces in the management team

A complex system lives at the same time in two worlds: external and internal. Things happen both visibly and hidden, below the surface. Both of these complex worlds are present at the same time in the system and they form together a tense relationship. The visible world represents the commonly accepted ways to operate and what is desirable to strive for. The world below the surface, in turn, consists of things that are kept muted and of which there may not even be awareness. The latter can be identified, for example, with the help of these questions:

- What are we not allowed to talk about in the management team?
- What is left unsaid in the management team meetings?
- Who in the team has the strongest impact and power of influence? Why?
- Whose words are ignored? Why?

Systemic Idea 2: Paradoxes are compulsory

Systems thinking also offers a perspective that allows the management team to reach a deeper level in its conversations. Systems thinking challenges how to deal with and to live in coexistence with various paradoxes of life. A paradox is, by definition, a seemingly unreasonable claim or statement, which is not true but leads to conflict. Paradoxes in organizations are in general expressions of expectations, which combined form an impossible equation. Here is a list of the most typical paradoxes that concern the management team.

Think in the long run – Cash in on the results
Cut the costs – Enhance morale and boost welfare
Reduce staff – Improve team spirit
Be flexible – Respect the rules
Cooperate – Compete

Decentralize – Keep control
Keep costs down – Do not compromise on quality
Stay close – Keep distance
Be confident – Be humble
Innovate – Avoid errors

Internal conflicts are part of the nature of paradoxes and they can easily cause inactivity. Through systems thinking, paradoxes become a significant driving force for change. By identifying and exploring together in your team the inherent tensions of paradoxes, you will add to your disposal the energies which accumulated in paradoxes. The paradoxes do not disappear, nor are they resolved. Instead, you increase your understanding of systemic forces that affect your management team and your work. This, in turn, opens up totally new opportunities for collaboration in a Stellar Team.

TRY THIS: Understand the paradoxes of your management team

1. Each one of you picks independently three paradoxes from Table 2.1. that in your opinion affect most the success of your team. The selection is based on the tension generated by the attraction of both of the two extremes. Both options can be seen in a positive light, but at the same time, they cannot be rationally implemented.
2. Write down on a flip chart the individual choices and then select the three most supported paradoxes for your group level process.
3. Describe the commonly identified tensions, with the aim of understanding the hidden forces. Appreciate every opinion and explore together.
4. Discuss, what effect all the identified tensions have had. In which daily situations do they appear? Important: the target is to understand, not to change. As understanding increases, change becomes inevitable.

Systemic Idea 3: Spontaneity creates miracles

Change can be induced by someone just acting in a new way. This is called the miracle of spontaneity. When someone breaks out from customary and safe ways, he or she forces the surrounding system to reorganize itself. This person creates spontaneously a new system, which works better than the previous one (Williams 2002).

- Change in any part of the system, irrespective of whether the change is spontaneous or not, means changes in the entire system. Although the end result may be unclear for the management team, it is worth taking risks and making changes. The system has a chance to change.

Systemic Idea 4: Resistance belongs to systems

All living systems accept what seems to be appropriate and nourishing, but reject what is strange or seemingly unnecessary. Living systems are generally suspicious of the unidentified. When a man resists a change he sees the current state as a better option than the risks associated with a new state. In all of us there is a big „no%always ready to be activated in a new situation, in particular if the situation somehow threatens the *status quo*.

- Change resistance is a sign that the kinetic energy, which is used for resistance, is waiting for reorientation. Seeking imbalance is worth trying in the management team. That is a risk worth taking. The change will start to take place with the appearance of an imbalance.

Sharing change experiences reduces stress and makes one feel better. Talking about bothersome and unclear issues attaches mental tensions to integrities that are more under control and more understandable as a whole. This kind of attachment improves human performance. The meaningless becomes meaningful and things become ordered.

- Each member of a management team is a human being. Would it now be time to admit this, and begin to confess your own uncertainty and ignorance also to your colleagues in the management team? Talking about these issues makes things visible – and talking helps.

Systemic Idea 5: Everything affects everything in a system

In management teams we often meet people who are happy with being mostly, or even exclusively, in the role of an observer. Observers do not say anything, they are only making interpretations in their own minds. Each part of the system, even the observers, affect the system and the system affects them. At the same time, the system also affects the objectivity of observers. If ideas and perspectives arise in the observerŝ mind and these remain unspoken, information is deposited in the hidden layers of the system. Even silence has its influence, as much as any commentary.

- If there is to be an observer in the management team, this has to be agreed specifically. The observer has an obligation to place all of his or her findings at the teamŝ disposal.
- Everyone influences the actions of the management team, because everyone is a part of the management team system. What kind of impact are you making on the system? What kind of change could you make in your behaviour system already in the next meeting?

Systemic Idea 6: Leadership renews itself constantly

In systems thinking leadership is based on connections between people. Members of a team or a community affect the leadership and are, at the same time, part of the expression of leadership. The leadership is also independent of formal status. In a system everyone has a chance to influence (to take leadership) and to be influenced (to take followship).

- Formal director positions are needed, too. However, it is useful to weaken the hierarchies and control that are constructed in the system. A formal leader position is restrictive and deactivating.
- Give the opportunity for leadership that exists in every group, and which is free of rank and status.

Systemic Idea 7: Control is an illusion

No one is capable of controlling a system and all its associated variables. Analysing a system has its limitations, too, because of its dynamic nature and constant movement. For this reason, it is not useful to explain a system, but instead, to study it to obtain fresh understanding of the system, and to gain wisdom for the decision-making process. An iceberg is not entirely visible and respectively, the hidden layers of a system are primarily not rationally explicable. Behind the logic lies the level of emotions. Sometimes as things get stuck, it is useful to ask, which emotions are connected to different things, where do these emotions come from and what do they really tell us?

- ÂUncontrollabilityÊis a part of the learning and development which takes us towards a Stellar Team.
- ÂIncompletenessÊis a good starting point, because then the management team will be doggedly on its path of renewal and development.

Systemic Idea 8: Change is a constantly changing phenomenon

Systems theory offers the management team useful insights for change discussions and change management practices. Systemic ideas on self-organizing and change dynamics merit joint reflection in the management team. Any system has three essential features marking a self-organizing tendency.

1. **Prerequisite for renewal**
   Renewal is produced only by a system that is out of balance. Alignment and stability, in themselves, do not create anything new. Instead, tensions and polarization keep the system energetic.

   - How does the management team make sure that it will not fall into complacency but rather constantly strive towards energies that keep the system evolving?
   - How does the management team call the obvious into question?

2. **Need for energy loss**
   Energy loss comes from disorder, mistakes, lost information, idle chitchat. The closer we get to chaos, the more energy loss will occur. We need a lot of experimentation and trials – wrong operations and other irrational actions – in

order to finally find the most rational way to act. If we desperately try to discard all energy loss, we will only be pseudo-effective. Every mistake, error or failure, big or small, produces important information.

- When was the last time you shared your personal flops and failures in your management team?
- How does your management team ensure that there is sufficient time for off-the-record talking and get-together?

3. Choices are irreversible

Every system will come to a crossroads and will need to make choices. Choices cannot be predicted, as they are always selected according to the situation. Choices are also irreversible and form part of the history of a system. At the same time, irreversibility creates order in the system. Change is a built-in feature in the system, change leads from one choice to another.

- Isnʼt it time to put an end to plans that reach too far? Every decision and associated impacts produce, in any case, more understanding, which also adds more precision to plans.
- Isnʼt it be time to take an interest in what effect your management team produces on your environment – on your own working community and on your customers?

Systems oriented management team enables Superproductivity

In complex interaction systems, the mission of leadership is to create conditions for different encounters and learning opportunities, because complex systems between people cannot be controlled, and events cannot be planned in detail in advance. (Marion and Uhl-Bien 2001). A good application of this, is the concept of *Superproductivity*. The concept was introduced in 2007, by Dr J.T. Bergqvist, who is known, amongst other things, as a former member of the Executive Board of Nokia.

Superproductivity is a state which triggers by means of innovation productivity growth that exceeds expectations. A company is a system where human interaction exerts a strengthening impact both on energy levels and on a spirit of innovation. That is why the creation of the right atmosphere is the prerequisite for Superproductivity. This atmosphere is constructed in daily encounters between people, mostly through every-day and supposedly meaningless behaviour models. They may include, for example, listening, giving space to others, apologizing or encouraging people to celebrate even their small successes.

A management team of five members arrived for their meeting on time, a little bit busy perhaps, but prepared, and they took care of their responsibilities as members of that team. The productivity of this team can be described by a formula, in which each member of the management team brought themselves to the setting having a value of 1:

$1 \times 1 \times 1 \times 1 \times 1 =$ ***1***

For a second time, the members of the management team arrived at their meeting tired, busy, ill-prepared and, above all, displaying a lack of respect towards other members and the team̂s work. At this meeting, the members did not participate wholeheartedly. Now the value of their individual contribution can be described in the formula as 0.8:

$$0.8 \times 0.8 \times 0.8 \times 0.8 \times 0.8 = \textbf{0.328}$$

Next time, the members of the team came to the meeting alert, focused, very well-prepared and, above all, armed with an appreciative mind-set towards other members and the work of the management team. The mind-set was obvious even before the start of the meeting as they chatted and greeted each other. Now the individual̂s value in our formula is 1.2:

$$1.2 \times 1.2 \times 1.2 \times 1.2 \times 1.2 = \textbf{2.49}$$

TRY THIS: Can you make a difference?

You can try small steps at your next meeting that will raise the value above the standard of 1.0.

- What would be your small steps? – Greeting, a friendly word, thanks, feedback, smile, eye contact, an acknowledgement, listening, a comment, a focus in cooperation . . .?
- How could you meaningfully spread these small steps to the others?

Systems thinking leads us to reflect on individual skill level and momentary mental agility, but particularly on relations between team members.

- What are the relationships between members of the management team like?
- Do you notice between some members a relationship that produces a value higher than 1.0?
- Do you recognize relations where the figure goes below 1.0?
- How do you actively influence the quality level of relations in your team? How do you influence interactive relationships within your team? What could you do differently to make relations superproductive?

Success factors of the Stellar Team

What does a top management team look like? Over the years, we have had a number of discussions on this theme with various management teams. Each management team is a system of its own, with its own disciplines. What are the characteristics, which a team should possess, in order to be justly described, as top, excellent, unique, efficient and effective – a true Stellar Team?

In general teams promote very similar ideals. Important things are e.g. common goal, an open and confidential atmosphere, an appreciative attitude towards team members, working according to common rules, the possibility to use oneŝ own strengths in order to achieve a common goal, a good atmosphere and so on.

A number of researchers into teamwork and management teams have tried to model what a successful working experience looks like. We took on the task of reading half a dozen different theories, each one with its own emphases. Our selected thought-leaders are Rubin, Plovnik and Fry (1977), Katzenbach and Smith (1993), LaFasto and Larson (2001), Hackman (2002), Lencioni (2002) and Wageman et al. (2008). We cross-tabulated the characteristics of top teams, and arrived at a basis for an effective and resourceful team (Table 2.1).

The message of researchers and developers begins to condense. In our summary table we have described the characteristics quantitatively: the first have received the most support from the researchers. If we still compress the classification, we eventually come to three fundamental qualities. A team appears successful and well-functioning when:

Table 2.1 Seven factors of a Stellar Team

	A	B	C	D	E	F
(1) Clear task and distinct objective	X	X		X	X	X
(2) Appropriate mind-set – commitment – right people – individuals want to learn – accountability		X	X	X		X
(3) Complementary competencies – diversity in know-how – problem solving skills – leadership skills		X	X	X		X
(4) Relationships for cooperation – mutual trust – willingness and ability to cooperate – courage to face conflicts	X		X	X	X	
(5) Guiding framework – purposeful processes – well-defined roles and job descriptions – supportive structures	X			X		X
(6) Organizational culture that values cooperation			X	X		X
(7) Support from professional coaches enabled			X			X

A: Rubin, Plovnik and Fry (1977), B: Katzenbach and Smith (1993), C: LaFasto and Larsson (2001), D: Hackman (2002), E: Lencioni (2002) and F: Wageman et al (2008).

- Cornerstones of operations are in place (factors 1 and 5). The operation is guided by goal and supported by structures.
- Members of the team are committed to the collaboration and want to learn together (factors 2, 3 and 4).
- Focus is outside the team. The management team wants deliberately to influence the organizational culture, and know they need an external „challenger‰ for their own development (factors 6 and 7).

Towards the star

The factors that make for a Stellar Team have now been compiled. We have taken into account the results of the most relevant parts of research and background theories, and added elements from our experience in the development of various management teams. This book is constructed on a frame of reference, which we have shaped out of the factors of the Stellar Team (Figure 2.1).

Figure 2.1 The guiding star

A Stellar Team is developed, point by point, finally forming a whole, which is more than the sum of its parts. We will dig deeper into all the elements of the Stellar Team in this book. However, we shall first clarify the concepts of Primary Goal and Secondary Goal in our figure of guiding star.

The two levels: Primary and Secondary Goals

The construction of our symbolic guiding star shows the idea of two types of goals: Primary Goals and Secondary Goals. The Secondary Goals are the five points of the star while Primary Goals form the cortex and the core of the star.

The Secondary Goals consist of all the visible forms of operations and focuses of attention, which the management team discusses in their daily work. The management team talks about **external stakeholders** – the most important of them are customers – and **internal stakeholders**, which include, for example, signals coming from within the organization. The **course** has to be planned, that means for example, strategy discussions, focus and the objectives of management team. An essential focus of attention is **success indicators**, because ultimately, the management team is looking for results and profits. Everything is based on constant care for smooth cooperation on a daily basis, which is guaranteed by functioning **meeting procedures**.

These all are important goals. Based on our experience we can say that, nowadays, the majority of the management teams primarily direct their attention to the above mentioned Secondary Goals.

WAKE UP! IF ATTENTION IS MERELY ON OPERATING ACCORDING TO SEC-ONDARY GOALS, THE MANAGEMENT TEAM CAN NEVER TAKE ADVANTAGE OF ITS FULL POTENTIAL.

A significant part of the potential in the management team will not be used, if the Primary Goals are left unattended. Therefore, even if the management team's strategies and internal processes were finely polished, and even if echoes of the voices of customers and subordinates could be heard clearly in the meetings of the management team – that simply would not be enough. We need more – **we need to sit up and pay attention to the Primary Goals of management team!**

The Primary Goals form the team's treaty: a declaration of cooperation, unity and mutual assistance. The Primary Goals direct the attention to the team and, to how it works as a team. The cortex of the guiding star is divided into four sectors, which build up the Primary Goals. The elements are visible and directly affect the functioning of the team. The core issues are then:

• How is **diversity** within the team taken advantage of? How are differences taken into account, concerning both knowledge and in particular, action styles? In **conflict** situations, does the management team know how to „argue constructively‰

- How do the members of management team **cooperate** with each other – at meetings and, especially, between the meetings?
- How do the members of management team give and receive **feedback**? What is the feedback culture like?

In the symbol of the Stellar Team, the core of the star sets **resilience** as an additional team objective. Individual abilities help to recover from disruptions caused by change and they form the basis for the team's ability to adapt to change. Finally, at the heart of the core are individual-level commitment and team level trust, which together function as the energy generator for the Primary Goals.

Figure PS.1 The guiding star summary

Core of Part I: thinking, systems and guiding star

In this book we will undertake a metaphorical journey to the stars. This symbolizes the development from an ordinary management team into a Stellar Team, which elevates its operation up to a new level of results. In Part I we examined the underlying patterns of thought and background theories of management team development.

A significant change in the operating environment will challenge the organization and its adaptation management. Now there is a need for new, healthy thinking. A systemic perspective leads to consider the well-worn work in the management team in a new way. Every new idea works like a wing beat of a butterfly. Everything affects everything else.

The more the management team focuses on the Primary Goals, the better and the more efficiently it will also be able to implement the Secondary Goals.

- The journey to the stars commences when the management team renews its thinking.
- Systemic or holistic thinking changes the approach to management and to collaboration within the management team.
- Developing into a Stellar Team does not just mean controlling and adding colour to black and white thinking. The Stellar Team means enabling.

Part II

Secondary Goals are the launch pad

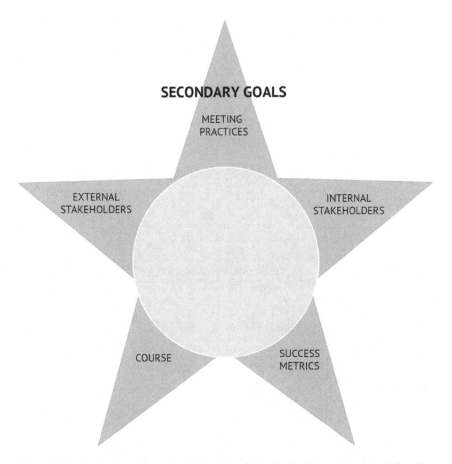

Figure PII.1 Goals: Secondary Goals describe **what** a Stellar Team does in collaboration and **why** it cooperates

3   The course is set

MANAGEMENT TEAM VERTIGO

Symptom: Reflexive focus on operational objectives

Management team vertigo is an embarrassing discomfort, which often arises if *management team swell* is treated by rising too quickly to the top of a viewing tower. This syndrome is easy to explain with a down-to-earth metaphor. If a man is used to working on the ground, a rapid transition to the heights will easily cause a feeling of dizziness. He will cling automatically to the nearest support. For a member of management team this means the following: If you are used to working on an operational basis, a rapid transition to strategic level will cause uncertainty, and so, at meetings, you quickly grab onto your own unitŝ operational issues. However, this emergency relief will only take you from bad to worse, because of operational focus and you will easily end back to the painful *management team swelling*.

Care instructions in Appendix 2: ÂSelf care guide for management teamsÊ

A management team needs a mission of its own

What is the purpose of existence for a management team? What would it be like without any management team at all? What is the added value that the management team together generates, and that is not possible for each member to achieve separately?

Our observations on the life of a management teamŝ mission are quite unpleasant. The company mission is clear, but the management team mission is very seldom defined. The management team works without any mutual discussion of its mission, or even less, without crystallizing the purpose of its existence. This is sad. When a management team clarifies its mission, it strengthens the basis of its operations and empowers the team.

The management team has a big responsibility, as it directs the focus of the collaboration in the whole company. Imagine two management teams, which represent the extremes of implementing the company mission. The first one indulges in strategic discussions, the sharing of ideas for future guidelines and decision-making concerning the whole organization. The second one focuses on individuals and on monitoring the performance of business units or divisions. The meetings consist mainly of the reporting of individual responsibilities.

These extremes also describe individual attitudes to work and the significance of the management team. The following is an example of a management team meeting.

Peter, the CEO in an expert organization, often spoke loudly and passionately about the importance of work with customers. The phrase „the customer is number one%was very familiar to the management team. This perceived customer value had affected the joint action of the management team. The nine members were hardly ever present at the same time in their meetings. The constant justification for absence was „an appointment with a customer%and no one questioned it. The organization focused on customers, but the culture had a very weak foundation. The management team had mostly become a club for patting each other on the back. The customers were important for them, which was undoubtedly right. However, management team values could also be different.

In a common development process the management team decided to retain the position of the customer as number one whilst, at the same time, investing in the development of the team. They made a common agreement that team meetings were to be their number one priority in their calendars, and everyone committed to put an effort into looking for other alternatives for customer appointments. The habits of the management team were changed, and the team was able to focus on their own basic mission – all together.

The best mission is a defined mission

The management team needs a common idea of its primary task and mission as a core of its existence. As management teams are different, there is no standard mission available. Depending on the size of the company, the stage of the life cycle and the hierarchy level, the mission of a management team takes a variety of different forms. To support discussion of the mission, we have developed a quadrant table, which describes different approaches (Figure 3.1). The table is based on two continuums: (1) operational vs. strategic dimension and (2) people vs. task oriented working focus. Their combinations form four different types of mission: spokesmen, problem solvers, developers and decision makers.

The missions shown in Figure 3.1 must not be understood as black and white. It is clear that every management team has to make decisions, to develop, to solve problems and to communicate. Essential in the discussion is the focus:

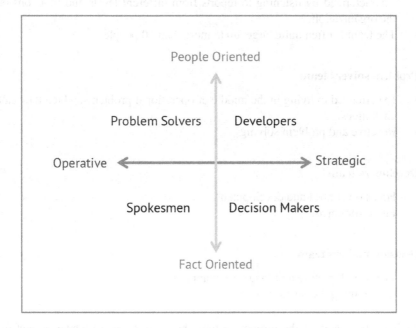

Figure 3.1 Different missions of the management team

Where is the emphasis of the work in the management team? The most basic question is on the horizontal axis: Is the management team primarily operational or strategic? If the focus is on the strategic side, the main question is, does the team concentrate primarily on development or on making decisions on guidelines for the future.

If the management team͡s mission is primarily to focus on development, then their agenda consists of numerous strategic development projects, their monitoring and implementation evaluation. This type of management team also invests common time in development and recruits development-oriented individuals into the team.

Similarly, if the core operation of the management team is strategic decision-making, they need to ascend to the observation tower to look out from that perspective and towards the future. The management team is then primarily deciding on guidelines and showing directions.

If the primary function of the management team is operational, we move to the left side of the table. A problem solving management team focuses on the problems of the future and invests time in finding various solution options. The problems are usually linked, directly or indirectly, to the „human problems%found in business units or teams.

Spokesmen team

•   Focus primarily on keeping its members aware of what is happening in different parts of the organization.

- Characterized by listening to reports from different levels and functions of the organization.
- The team is often quite large, up to more than 10 people.

Problem solvers team

- Experienced in living in the middle of operational problems, which they call challenges.
- Reactive and problem solving

Developers team

- Focus on control and development.
- Future-oriented.

Decision makers team

- The overall picture and long term planning.
- Guide lining the operations.

Defining the focus of the mission is fatal, because it has a broader impact on management team cooperation. At its best, the mission of a management team sets clear guidelines for:

- structure
- principles of membership
- frequency of meetings
- duration and agenda of meetings
- ways of working

How about a conversation: the core of your management team? Try it – it is surely worth it.

Make your mission alive

Thus, the management team needs a mission of its own. We have created some examples of missions and placed them in our quadrant table. These examples come from our conversations with various management teams. In following figures we have circled the focus area in which each management team works, on the basis of its own mission.

  The examples above show that the focus of the mission varies depending on the situation and the management team itself. Finding the right focus brings clarity and steers team action. When the mission of the management team is communicated to the rest of the organization, clarity will increase even further.

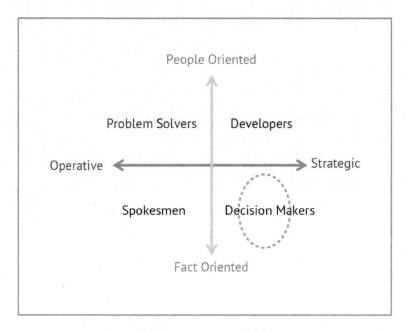

Figure 3.2 „We lead tomorrowŝ business with todayŝ decisions. We choose the direction and lead staff within the framework of Group Policy to create economic value.‰

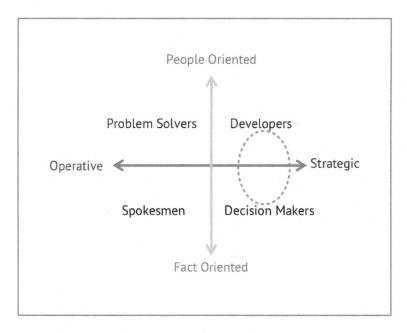

Figure 3.3 „We head to the future and guide the strategic development of our company. We make customer-driven decisions throughout the entire sales organization.‰

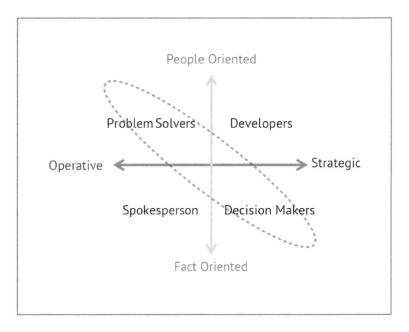

Figure 3.4 „We show direction and make choices. We ensure optimal results by focusing on direction, speed and resources.‰

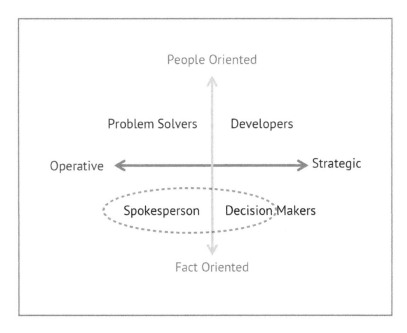

Figure 3.5 „We act as a conduit for information sharing and we make decisions across distribution channels and responsibility areas.‰

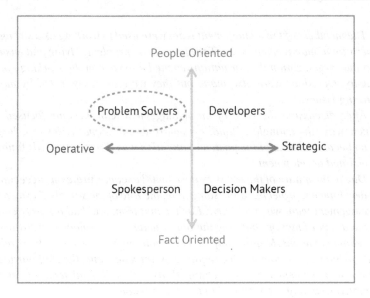

Figure 3.6 „We take care of the internal functioning of our organization and its capacity for renewal. We create conditions for internal cooperation and efficiency.‰

The process of defining the management team mission widely influenced the management system. The team agreed on a change from an operative management team to a strategic decision-making body. They drew the change in the table as in the Figure 3.7.

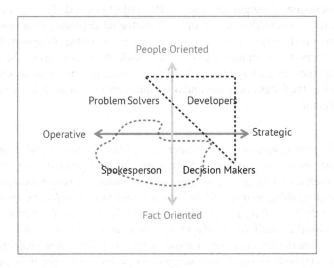

Figure 3.7 Transformation from operative to strategic decision-making body

The members of the management team were used to working as a strongly operational management team. They focused on problem solving and ensuring that organizational information reached everyone in the working community. Decisions were also made but they were often overruled by more burning issues.

After discussion the core of the management team became focused in a new way (the triangle). Handling separate operational cases in a large team became a thing of the past, and attention was directed towards future-orientated development.

Due to the nature of the industry it was vital to concentrate on succeeding in development projects. At the same time, the role of the so-called extended management team was redefined. Earlier that team had had a purely communicational function, but now the old structure was replaced by strategic development teams. Membership in those teams was not based on hierarchical position but on competence required. At the same time, the configuration of the management team was changed, as the traditional team of representatives no longer correlated to the new mission.

Make your guiding star visible

In addition to a mission, every management team needs an inspirational vision. After having defined the mission the management team should continue with the discussion of their guiding star, i.e. the vision. What kind of management team do we want to be? How do we know that we have accomplished that? Which factors show us that we are keeping to the right course?

The discussion of the guiding star – called objectives in daily language – leads attention to joint direction and it strengthens the prerequisites to develop themselves into a real Stellar Team. A common goal is one of the obligatory factors in a Stellar Team. If a common goal does not guide the operations of the management team, they are merely toying. Sometimes there may be too many objectives, which makes the focus disappear and it becomes impossible to direct your energy to the essential.

A management team in creative business had the practice of updating their strategic guidelines annually. Each year, the management team created great outlines for the strategy. There were a number of PowerPoint presentations describing their spearhead projects and core areas for the upcoming year. In their coaching group they woke up to the fact that these great plans hardly lived in daily life of the management team, although each project was systematically assigned to team members. Quite a few projects burdened everybody so much, that many other projects were not tight enough and this resulted mainly in feelings of inadequacy.

The management team had an intensive discussion and they noticed, that they were concentrating on planning actions but leaving common objectives aside. Hence, the team members decided to change their ways: they started to seek focus. After a tough debate they ended up with three objectives concerning the whole organization. In the beginning, speaking „target language‰felt strange and difficult but it freed their thoughts. The question „What shall we do?‰was replaced by „What shall we achieve?‰i.e. they moved from action planning to goals, which was a remarkable step in their team development. The debate became crystallized.

- Our Focus: We are going to implement the three objectives concerning the whole organization by the end of the accounting period.
- Our Unity: The management team will act outside the meeting room in a uniform and exemplary manner.

The management team even attached assessments to both objectives, which strengthened the guiding effect. The operations of the management team were transformed from the monitoring of multiple projects to managing the goals.

Goal heat is dangerous

A common goal is vital for a Stellar Team. Many organizations exist for goals, and pre-set goals guide management teams, too. Very well, as long as you take care that the pre-set goals do not function as blinkers, which prevent us from seeing the constantly evolving world around. A common goal may, at its worst, become an absolute, destroying all the positive characteristics of a goal. This causes something that we call hyper-keenness.

Goal heat is a state where a management team – or any individual – becomes too strongly fixed on a goal. The sensitivity to perceive and react becomes narrowed, when you try solely to see things that are in harmony with your goals. A too strong goal orientation limits thinking, which limits acting. The more detailed and precise the goals are, the more they direct our focus and, at the same time, they may exclude perhaps very remarkable perceptions.

Exact prediction in this complex world is impossible, so the management must not direct all its energy into concretizing the objectives. „The most adaptable to change will survive‰sounds valid and reasonable concerning management teams. (The origin of that clever quote is unknown, although it is commonly attributed to Darwin, but without proof.) The odds for success improve, the more agile the management team is in reacting to the changes in its environment. This will prevent goal blindness.

The goal functions in a positive way, as a person or a team is committed to the goal and they have the required competence to achieve it. The probability of achieving the goal increases even more, if we ensure that there is no opposing goal. The function of a goal very much depends on the way it is defined. While reading the following thoughts, it may be useful to consider the quality of goal language in your team.

The book *Beyond Goals*, edited by David Clutterbuck et al., significantly analyses the relativity of goals. Here we have summarized the essential observations of the book.

(1)   SMART goal narrows too much!

Many organizations and management teams are used to defining their goals in line with the SMART model. This model states that a good way to set goals is to ensure that they are specific, measurable, actionable, realistic and timely. However, SMART gives just one limited description of the diversity of goals. What would happen in your thinking if the goal were to be considered in relation to four continuums?

> Short term – Long term
> Concrete – Abstract
> Towards – Away from
> Performing – Learning

(Grant 2007)

These goal continuums challenge the SMART hypothesis. SMART may indeed not be very suitable for long term goals. Sometimes it is better to leave abstract goals without metrics, as they are not measurable. Additionally, there are even situations where the goals aim at keeping up the status quo.

A SMART goal is suitable only for the last continuum, which emphasizes performance. The difference between performance and learning goals is anyway clear: the focus is either on the end result or on process.

- Performance goal of a management team: What shall we do next?

  - Let's build an online store! (end result)

- Learning goal of a management team: How shall we learn to expand our business?

  - Let's build an online store! (process)

Both expressions use goal language but obtain a different impact. Let the goal guide your mind – but which one of the examples above works better for you?

(2)   Goal may weaken morality?

The objectives may also be related to an unethical perspective. *Goal heat* can lead to the pursuit of the goal at any cost. Tension is very typical between the common objective of the management team and the individual or business unit level objective. If the attention moves to individual interests and personal incentives, you end up very fast in a grey area. People stop talking about mutually essential things, because sharing might bring about an undesirable effect as regards their own incentives. The objectives serve only their own personal interest – at any price.

(3)   Goals may prevent learning

A goal that is too narrow and too specific may lead the team to place all its eggs in one basket and perform the necessary operations according to the pre-set goal. Many researchers (e.g. Ordóñez et. al 2009) have said, that performance-orientated culture inhibits learning, and at the same time, the basic conditions for sustainable development are not strengthened. If performance leads to measurable objectives, how do we ensure at the same time, that learning takes place? By paying attention, not to the goal, but to the journey – that is, by asking, how we did it, how we thought of doing it and how we acted. Learning occurs when we become aware of how we are acting. Learning is „a relatively permanent change in behaviour‰ and that is why the Stellar Team must not focus only on performance goals.

(4)   Goals may lead to over-performing

Setting a goal adds commitment, but at the same time, it can also generate in certain situations undue pressure. We start to speak „should language‰ Internal or external „musts‰ rarely bring the very best out of an individual. A relaxed approach will support in exceeding previous results as regards the quality of the performance. If pursuing the goal results in undue pressure, success in the game will be poor.

(5)   Linearity of goals is rare

In a laboratory you can minimize the influence of background variables but in real life this is not possible. In the short term, detailed objectives are justified, but the more complex the entity, the more questionable it is to adhere to strictly defined objectives. The linear belief in the background behind objectives is not always true. „We shall change from state A to state B by focusing on a limited object C‰ It sounds plausible, but often the complexity of the world prevents that simplification from becoming true. Otherwise, every management team could simply decide: we shall improve our operating profit by focusing on price increase!

(6)   Controlling through goals is an illusion

The ultimate aim of a goal is to guide the behaviour of individuals. The goal always contains the dimension of control. However, life is a complex entity, consisting of so many variables that it cannot be controlled. Traditional goal thinking can work only in appropriately simple situations. For example, on a car trip, parents can control the children̂s fighting in the back seat for a while, by providing them with a goal-oriented task: who can see the most road signs beginning with letter C on this trip.

Something similar may work in the management team, too, but probably not for very long. ;)

Deepening goal thinking

As a basis for creating an inspiring vision, we will have a look at the connection between motivation and happiness.

Edward Deci and Richard Ryan, professors at the University of Rochester, released the theory in the 1980s that divided people into being intrinsically and extrinsically motivated. Intrinsically motivated people are driven by the freedom of self-determination, awareness of knowledge and efficacy, and connection to other people. All these are subjectively experienced. Correspondingly, extrinsically motivated appreciate externally visible factors, such as money, fame and glory. Thereafter, the professors divided 246 students in their experiment into two groups, depending on whether they valued intrinsically or extrinsically defined achievements. Both groups were supposed to attain their goals to some extent.

The follow-up showed a clear difference between the two groups.

- Students who were intrinsically motivated and who had reached their goals had improved their quality of life significantly, factors of well-being had been amplified and negative emotions – anxiety and stress – had declined. Subsequently too intrinsic motivation continued to increase well-being significantly and decrease mental ill-being.
- Students who were extrinsically motivated and reached their goals did not experience any improvement in well-being but mental ill-being increased instead. Hence the extrinsically motivated achieved the desired fame and fortune but consequently with increased ill-being!

(Ryan et al. 2009)

We have learned that reward and punishment are the real elements that lead to success and happiness, but from the above facts it can be concluded that even the quality of the goal is influential. Already in the days of antiquity a philosopher, who was not at all acquainted with psychology, Aristotle by name, stated:

Happiness, whether consisting in pleasure or virtue, or both, is more often found with those who are highly cultivated in their minds and in their character, and have only a moderate share of external goods, than among those who possess external goods to a useless extent but are deficient in higher qualities.
(https://en.wikiquote.org/wiki/Aristotle)

– What could this mean in a modern management team?

COMPARE: How do we obtain motivation and well-being?

- *An extrinsically motivated management team sets a financial goal and works hard to reach it. The stress is followed by success, which causes a short-lived feeling of happiness. The impact of incentives is soon displaced by bigger goals and the challenges of the next quarter or financial year – and the stress grows stronger and stronger . . .*
- *An intrinsically motivated management team sets alongside a financial goal also* **Primary Goals** *with keywords, e.g.* **freedom, feeling of know-how** *and* **connection to other people***. This team feels they control and are able to influence their own lives; they produce results that are important for them personally and create purposeful action for other people. Intrinsic motivation generates well-being that is real and sustainable.*

How to follow your star?

The goal controls action. The management team functions best when all its members embrace the goals of the organization sufficiently and act according to them. People are different, but succeeding in an important objective is rewarding. Many people are inspired by goals, when they are forced to think about new ways of working. A good goal offers them the most interesting challenge: How would I implement this? The goals drive development, as they give rise to changes and discomfort. Some argue that real pursuit of goals should include some passionate and even maniac-like characteristics.

A management team of an industrial group had a series of discussions of common goals. Finally, the management team defined its own values, which would guide it in all aspects of goal-setting:

Our goals inspire us

We do not settle for trivial achievements, but we are inspired by inspiring and almost impossible goals. Thatŝ why we have together defined common goals that are in our experience significant and meaningful. Aligned action inspires us. In addition, each of us has unique goals that are connected to individual responsibilities. Also we combine all our goals to achieve something more important than career.

Our goals create commitment

It is natural for us to work together and be actively involved in this complex and rapidly changing world. That is why we invest our time in the management team to discuss differing opinions, so that each and every one of us will commit to act in an aligned manner, according to our common goals.

Our goals connect us to each other

We have defined our objectives in a fascinating way both in overall view and in impressive detail. Our goals create in us a strong desire to achieve those goals. Our goals build in us the necessary courage and they strengthen our mutual loyalty. Each and every one of us operates without any hesitation, side by side, towards the achievement of the goals.

Our goals are right

Our goals are in line with our true values and important personal expectations of life. We identify behaviours, which fight against our goals, and we seize upon those openly. We know it is right to do what we are doing.

REFLECT TOGETHER: Make your star shine

1. *What is the tiniest accomplishment that could make us jump for joy? (Figuratively – jumping for joy is definitely impossible for a management team member who is older than 6 years.)*
2. *What could be such an enormous and inspiring goal that we would not be able to go to bed? (Figuratively – there may be sleeping disorders in your team anyway.)*
3. *Which significant success would be impossible for us in general? (Are there any such things, even figuratively – and if there are, how could they be accomplished anyway, if they were accomplishable?)*
4. *Concluded from previous answers: What turns on our glow and makes us enthusiastic and successful?*

Strategy makes your mind focused

Before you continue reading, try this:

Watch the video and count **how many times the basketball players in white pass the ball**. Duration of the video 1̂20 and the link is http://www.you tube.com/watch?v=vJG698U2Mvo, which you can also find in YouTube by searching for „Selective Attention Test‰
– So, please watch the video first!

Focusing means that a person first sets a goal and creates a clear destination, which then makes it natural to direct energy to the task. At the same time you can follow up progress and experience success. It also creates commitment to the task, as you are aware of having set the goal yourself instead of having followed extrinsic goals.

Focusing also means that a person after having set the goal, has an opportunity to immerse himself or herself in the task. The degree of attentiveness correlates directly to the strength of flow experience. Focus of mental energy and physical attention narrow down onto the goal and observations concerning the surrounding environment diminish or vanish totally. A splendid example of this is the basketball video mentioned above: a simplistic but challenging and focus-demanding task takes the attention. Thus, focused viewers, almost without exception, miss a remarkable incident. (Watch the video, if you want to know what it is!)

Individual significance of focus

Focusing or directing your attention saves brain capacity and influences your perceptions. Perception is rewarding and being rewarded influences your actions.

1. **Focusing helps us to cope**
   Human beings are capable of keeping 5–7 items at the same time in their so-called working memory. As the focus is sufficiently defined, working memory is not overloaded and thus attention is not disrupted.
2. **Focusing helps us to perceive**
   A common phrase says it: out of sight, out of mind. Missing the focus, i.e. the centre of attention, impacts perception and makes for an exact opposite order: out of mind, out of sight. Research in perception psychology shows indisputably that direction of attention impacts both the quality and quantity of perceptions.
3. **Focusing helps us to feel better**
   Every perception of focused action is rewarding. Seeking and finding something that is chosen to be the centre of attention, e.g. finding chanterelles amid undergrowth in the forest, causes a burst of dopamine in the brain of the seeker, resulting in a feeling of pleasure.
4. **Focusing helps us on to better results**
   The research shows that the joy of finding and a positive mood favourably influence the quality of almost any human action.
   A feeling of pleasure stimulates broad activation of the brain cortex, i.e. the capacity and knowledge in the brain become more accessible. A good mood often increases the intensity of action and, above all, the changes are measurable in results.

Focusing means that a person who is really engaged with a task sees only things that are related to the task. The perception gets sharper and the right things are recognized, even where they have not been perceived before. The findings are rewarding, and they accelerate the positive circle of flow.

Focus of the strategy

Now we will explore the connection between focus, strategy and its implementation. Focusing on the core of the strategy is quite a challenge for many organizations. If the focus of the strategy cannot be crystallized, one may end up with suspicions, which remind us of a wonderful slogan of a small but international business (not selling lenses): *We focus on everything!*

What do they want us to believe of their company? Based on that slogan, how do the employees strive to act differently to stand out in excellence from their competitors?

*Ollie told us he decided on a hot day, to surprise the management team by bringing ice cream to its meeting – although he himself never actually ate it. Ollie saw in the supermarket ice cream selection that there were far more than seven options to choose from. There were all kinds of flavours, berries and fruit, single and mixed, foreign and domestic origin, small boxes and giant bowls, big brands and local products. Ollie's working memory capacity was 5–7 items, so the focus on ice cream began to melt. Watching the countless options his working memory became overloaded and he ended up with **analysis paralysis**. Thus, Ollie turned away and decided to provide the management team with the same cookies as usual.*

WAKE UP! Focus anaemia causes analysis paralysis, which triggers giving up.

That's why the management team focuses in strategy only on one task, which has two phases:

1. First the management has to decide what they see as focused tasks of their own. This way they are able to direct their attention and energy to the right issues.
2. Then the management has to take care to communicate the focus to the organization so others are able to direct their attention and energy to the right issues.

EXERCISE: Find your focus

In case you feel often you are missing your focus then you need to train your brain to find it. This is how it goes.

1. The focus question is „What is the most important thing in this?‰ Ask yourself this question repeatedly, at the beginning of your day, working week, tasks, meetings, calendar reservations.

---

2. Sometimes it is useful to add a question: „What importance do I get from this?‰

3. Ask yourself every night: „Today what was the most important thing to me in doing this?‰

4. Go on with this programme for 8–12 weeks and ask yourself at the end: „What was the most important thing to me in this exercise programme?‰

5. In changing your brain and automatic thinking, it is important that you repeat the question sufficiently often and long enough. At some point you will notice that this focus question has become automatic in your thinking and you donÊt need to ask it consciously.

Before starting this programme ask yourself: „What is the most important thing to me in this?‰

4 Respect internal and external stakeholders

IMAGE DELUSION

Symptoms: Pathetic complacency and omnipotent hallucinations

Image delusion is a disease of numerous management team members. For such a patient membership of a management team has become an end in itself. The disease leads to taking action on the safe side and to distortion of focus. This in turn leads to the primary pursuit of retaining ones̃ own position in the management team, for as long as possible. *Image delusion* makes the patient feel a certain satisfaction, and before long, pathetic complacency begins to shine on the face of the patient.

Care instructions in Appendix 2: ̂Self care guide for management teamŝ

Customer experience is always right

Almost every company and corporation cultivates the word „customer%̇n their statements, activity reports, values and celebratory speeches. They promise to be customer centric, customer oriented and customer driven, to bring added value to customers, to exceed customer expectations and to exist for customers only. Every member of the management team is capable of producing customer talk even in deep sleep.

The facade of talking disappears very quickly if there is no action behind the words. Bain & Company conducted a study, which revealed that 80% of businesses believed that they were creating great experiences for their customers. However, only 8% of customers had the same opinion! Another study says that the main reason why customers cease to be customers or change their supplier, is disappointment in the way the company takes care of their customer relations (Löytänä and Kortesuo 2011).

Thus, customers do not chase after lower prices or better products, as directors so often delude themselves into believing. What is essential is how a company is able to meet the expectations of customers in all their operations.

Why do companies then fail in customer experience management? Authentic customer care is much more than beautiful words. The challenge is not easy. Succeeding does not become any easier with undefined responsibilities. There are only a few management teams that have a responsible Customer Experience Officer (CXO).

In a Stellar Team everyone takes care of customer experience. At best the example of the management team has spread so that every member of the organization, independent of position, has seized his or her responsibility for creating great customer experience. Siloed organizations, conflicting interests and diluted communication complicate collective accountability. Finally it is all about the culture and habits, where the management team can act as standard-bearer. It requires authentic commitment and individual decision-making to act in accordance with fine speeches.

The task of customer experience management is to maximize the value created by the company to its customers by providing relevant experiences for the customer. The customer then enters into the centre of all operations and helps the management team to look at operations through the eyes of customers.

TAKE THE CUSTOMER WITH YOU!

1. *Talks about customers and their significance steered towards action: a customer's representative was invited to the management team meeting. The agenda was modified so that the issues were related to activities at the customer interface. An outstanding customer brought important added value to the meeting. The members of the management team asked him directly about the effects of a variety of decisions, and they received important information about the brand image, which the customer had of the company and its operations.*

2. *It is not always possible to bring a customer to the meeting. Then there are other means. In another management team we agreed that throughout the meeting, one of the team members would take on the role of the client and would listen to the conversation in that role. This solution produced a lot of new perspectives in the summary at the end of the meeting. When the speeches were transitioned into action, and the customer's world became experiential knowledge, customers really began to live, as it were, in the management team.*

3. *A third management team added this template to meeting items, related to customer experience:*

    • *It was agreed that each member would interview a selected customer, aiming to get inside the mindscape of the customer and to explore the customer's way of thinking.*

- *In their subsequent meetings, in one selected issue, 2 or 3 members took the position of an interviewed customer.*
- *At the end of each meeting there was a discussion of the importance and added value, which this experiment with the customer's voice brought to the proceedings.*

Customer experience is redeemed at contact points

How do you get in touch with customer experience? The annual customer satisfaction survey is at most merely a glance in the rear mirror. The true state of customer experience does not become tangible with those surveys. Attention must be directed to the encounters between the customer and the company, that is where the experience is born.

When these points have been identified, they must be connected into the feedback process. The more the management team receives information on the functionality in „customer experience producing moments‰the stronger the voice of customer also in management team meetings will be. At the same time, asking for feedback is the beginning for continuing dialogue and the core of customer relationship management.

A Stellar Team runs an active dialogue with customers. The more the members of the team are interested in the customer's experience, the more their decision-making will be based on real information. Customers are not interested in the oratory of the Director General, but in what the company actually does for their benefit. The Stellar Team does not just make promises, but focuses predominantly on redeeming those promises.

Keep your eyes open

Cycles of change are becoming constantly faster. The more eyes watch the world around, the better the management team will be aware of development and the needs of customers. When considering accounts, it is often easy to ignore demanding customers, the customer of your customers, customers not yet won and those already lost.

Members of a Stellar Team look repeatedly through the customer's glasses. They are fascinated and they show it, when they observe the world. If the focus is only on the thoughts of existing customers, we are easily lulled into looking only at the present situation. The things we pay attention to, assume more importance. What if you observe life in the streets, in subways, in stores, coffee shops and restaurants? What is new? What can you see plenty of? What do you see only rarely?

The environment provides us with a continuous flow of tips and new ways of working that can be modelled in our everyday life. Tracking these weak signals is not a science, not magic, but the mobilization of creativity and vigilance within your organization. And letŝ not forget: your friends, children, grandparents and neighbours. They represent distinctive situations in life, a variety of backgrounds and ages, and often also different life values. What an interesting microcosm there is just next to you!

And thatŝ not all: how much more effectiveness will you get if every member of the management team guides their own team members to put the customerŝ glasses on and collect observations consciously from their own networks? The more observers, the better results.

Internal stakeholders must be taken seriously

SECRET SOCIETY PARALYSIS

Symptoms: Eyes turn inwards, environment suffers from information hunger

Secret society paralysis is a very typical disease in management teams. The disease is hardly noticeable within the team, but it silences all communications going out from the team. The management team becomes incapable of looking at the outside world and communicating their decisions. The team members turn their focus inward, and care only that each has the required information on issues for discussion and decision-making. *Secret society paralysis* culminates in mouths being firmly closed, when the team members come out of the meeting. In the background to this disease there can be a childlike ego-centrism and a distorted perception of information hunger within the working community.

Care instructions in Appendix 2: ÅSelf care guide for management teamsÊ

„People are the most important asset in our company%das been a well-known phrase in speeches and annual reports for ages. Successful companies do not only repeat phrases, but also act. A prime example of this is the Finnish escalator manufacturer Kone Corporation. According to Matti Alahuhta, CEO 2005–2014, the companyŝ success is driven by a working climate and encouragement, where the duty of management is to make the entire staff pursue common objectives.

> „Kone measures both customer satisfaction and employee satisfaction annually. These are the best indicators of how the business is going to evolve. Satisfied personnel are committed to the goals of the company‰

Alahuhta believes strongly in the importance of working climate and well-being at work. Logically „employees who will participate‰is also a so-called must win battle on the list of priorities in their strategy, which is defined every 3 years.

„ We have developed leadership more than before and at the same time imple-mented well-being programs for employees. All this shows that the caring and creative climate is real. This is one of our highest priorities‰

What Alahuhta says, is clearly confirmed by Merja Fischer in her Doctoral thesis *Linkages between Employee and Customer Perceptions in Business-to-Business Services – Towards Positively Deviant Performances* (Fischer 2012):

(1) Account managersÊperceptions of workplace climate predict customersÊ perceptions of service quality and
(2) field service engineersÊpersonal engagement predicts customersÊper-ceptions of quality.

The result of FischerÊs dissertation means, simplified, that happier employees serve customers so much better that even customers notice it.

WAKE UP! FORGET NOW ALL THOSE BEAUTIFUL WORDS ABOUT CUSTOMER SATISFACTION AS YOUR FIRST GOAL, IF EMPLOYEE SATISFACTION COMES ONLY SECOND.

More and more organizations are beginning to wake up to the need to take care of employee satisfaction, but real success requires clear action that expresses faith in the importance of well-being. Judging by the average results of climate surveys, one may think that management teams are not true believers but great sceptics.

Of course, a positive result will promote a positive atmosphere, but sceptics think that the positive effect will not work in the opposite direction. They believe that a positive atmosphere does not contribute to a positive result when using a human labour force. However, well-known animal studies in the last century have already shown that happier cows produce more milk. But there is still one more piece of research to be done: Are the more productive cows happier than the less productive?

EGG OR HEN?

Evaluate your organization. Which one is more significant for you: employ-ees make a better result because they are happier or employees are happier because they make a better result?

Board of directors – influential actor in the background

The board of directors is an essential stakeholder for the highest management team of an organization and the board has, at best, a great influence on the success of the company. The management team is authorized by the board of directors to operate according to the chosen strategy. As the difference between management team and board of directors is clear, it is easy for both of these functions of management to act to the benefit of the entire company.

A board of directors that is formed of external experts meets the requirements as regards the division of responsibilities, which are generally stated in legislation in most countries. If the board consists of employees of the company, it easily becomes the second management team of the CEO, just with a false name. Building a Stellar Team becomes essentially more difficult if the roles are easily mixed.

The board of directors is legally obliged to organize the operations of the company, supervise the managing director or CEO and promote the mission of the company. It is easier to take care of those basic tasks if the board works sufficiently apart from operational management. Building a Stellar Team becomes much easier when the management of operation and board of directors can cooperate closely.

An expert organization used to hold an annual strategy day for the management of the company and the board of directors, which consisted of external members. This common strategy process took advantage in a unique way of the companyŝ internal experience, as well as its external expertise.

A well-functioning board of directors provides a strongly influential background for the Stellar Team, as it takes an active role in shaping strategy and common future. When the division of responsibilities is clear and the practices have been agreed together, the board of directors and its members are a great resource for the operational management.

The board of directors in an expert organization agreed that its members could be in contact with the operational management team. The only rule was that the CEO should be informed before any management team members were contacted.

Board of directors meets the expectations of Stellar Team

When the board of directors and the management team cooperate, they both generate added value for the company. The board of directors supports the operational management at its best, when the board provides the management with

- backing for decision-making
- clarity of direction

- sparring ideas back and forth
- trust and freedom to operate
- intervention if necessary
- encouragement and faith in joint actions.

The support of the board required by the management team varies case by case. A „business as usual%situation means that the management primarily just expects industrial peace. Of course, even then the business connections of board members are highly valued for example as door openers or problem solvers, but how about in a tough situation, if strategy views differ between the management team and the board of directors? Then visionary support offered with the wisdom of a qualified board is a great help. „Wisdom%means in this case that the board particularly refrains from operational management, and a skilled management team knows, in turn, how to support the board so that it keeps strictly to the strategic side.

> *A board of directors had a very important role in setting goals for an international SME with some 100 employees. The board set a well-reasoned growth goal for the management. The management team had defined the focus of operation in cooperation with the board and so the implementation plan succeeded. The management team also valued the board because it held to the chosen line, although it even had good reasons to cash in on short-term gains. The management team felt that the entire company, from grass roots level to the board of directors, was striving in the same direction.*

5   Meeting practices in order

MEETING SYNDROME

**Symptoms: Working alone, frustration and
lack of inspiration**

The risk of *meeting syndrome* is very notable in every management team.
The disease takes two extreme forms. In the more common form the management team meets so often that the attention of the members is all the
time on preparations for the upcoming meeting. This means mostly planning and fine-tuning of one's own presentation. Once the meeting is over
one has to start preparation for the next meeting. *Meeting syndrome* does
not add to a sense of community as the thorough preparation needs to be
done alone and this of course reduces possibilities for discussion.

The second form of *meeting syndrome* is known by the name *hyper
agenda syndrome* and it appears at infrequently held meetings. The agendas
of those meetings are always long as your arm and clueless as regards logic.
Decisions are often made before the meeting, which therefore only acts as
a rubberstamp. *Meeting syndrome* makes management team members lose
the meaning of their actions, and enthusiasm evaporates. The most horrifying threat is severe frustration and an irresistible desire to get away.

Care instructions in Appendix 2: 'Self care guide for management teams'

Fully attended management team meetings are an essential prerequisite for the road
to the stars. A common time is, of course, not in itself enough; you have to find the
right methods within the available time frame to support the mission of the management team and the chosen route towards the stars. Many management teams have
tuned their meeting procedures into good shape. Technical and structural choices
are a good starting point. Paying attention to Secondary Goals will bring results.

Meeting practices and their functionality also reveal the operational performance of the management team. Meetings are all too often technical and concern individual accomplishments. They involve a lot of talk, mainly monologues,

in which the attention is on the rear mirror and monitoring past matters. When the focus of attention is on worthless issues and trivial points, all of the team's resources are not utilised. At worst, we are in the middle of a power struggle, in which adults in business suits are at war for domination of the playground, and everyone protects his or her sand castle till the very last moment.

Fine-tuning brains in the management team

The brain has three characteristics, which have a very big influence on human activity. We think we are in control, but the latest research shows that the brain's automated activities lead even the smartest of us, like puppets on a string. If we are aware of these automatized models, we will have the potential to affect the quality of management team meetings.

First: The brain is a machine for creating connections

The brain simplifies its work by putting things in „bunches‰ and at the same time it builds connections or associations that tune up our thinking. For instance, thinking of money leads, according to several studies, to a more independent and more selfish way of working.

> In a study, test subjects were subtly guided to create unconscious associations to money. Test subjects were not told to think consciously about quarterly goals, sales budget, structure of expenses, cash flow, incentive programmes nor any other normal financial topic taken from the usual agenda of a management team. Instead, a bundle of Monopoly banknotes left on the table or a screensaver showing banknotes turned thinking. Actually, even a very marginal money stimulus caused surprising effects on unconscious thinking and the visible behaviour of test subjects:

- Test subjects were given a complicated task, where they were, in the end, forced to ask for help. The money primed group tried to solve the problem on their own, for almost twice as long as the control group.
- The test organizer dropped, as if accidentally, a bundle of pens on the floor. Money primed test subjects helped less in picking up the pens than the control group.
- Test subjects were asked to place seats for themselves and for another person for a conversation, while the test organizer went out to fetch the other person. The money primed test subjects put the chairs at a distance of average 1.18 m, compared to the control group where the distance between the chairs was, on average, 0.80 m.

In the management team, we have good reason to be aware, that building cooperation requires more conscious effort from us, because money reduces natural willingness for cooperation and giving assistance.

Second: The brain presents most decisions by intuition

Intuitive solutions are born in the human mind all the time, without any specific priming. A study by John Bargh came to the estimate that 95% of our decisions are intuitive – while only 5% are objective and analytical.

Third: We have the brain of herd animals

Our brains control us primarily to act for the benefit of unity and survival of the herd. Therefore, we avoid controversy by nature, and we want to be good people to each other.

> WAKE UP! MEMBERS OF THE MANAGEMENT TEAM ARE THUS, (1) GOOD PEOPLE, (2) WHO ACT MAINLY BY INTUITION AND (3) WHOSE INTUITION IS MOSTLY PRIMED BY PROFIT, MONEY AND FIGURES.
> THAT'S WHY THEY AUTOMATICALLY STRIVE TO MOVE THOSE CHAIRS TO A DISTANCE OF 1.18 METERS, INSTEAD OF ACTING ACCORDING TO THEIR NATURE IN A HERD AND COMBINING THEIR BRAIN CAPACITY SYNERGISTICALLY.

This book wants to demonstrate that there is still hope. Research indicates that unselfishness is indeed one of our deepest human instincts, i.e. we choose with Hasty Intuition to help others. The study of face expressions (Keltner, et al. 1995) indicates that empathy is seen on the face before a conscious thought of empathy has arisen.

Good decisions are induced with questioning

When the management team wants to improve the quality of decisions, the challenge is not about time or cost. The most difficult challenge is how to create awareness that even the most experienced and capable directors are fallible. It is sometimes absolutely impossible to believe that I myself can make a mistake. But really, good strategy and sleek decisions are generated in a tight and organized decision-making process, not out of individual geniality. A Stellar Team has a culture that favours open discussions and this leads to a high quality of decisions.

> *How does my own interest affect my thinking?*
> It is easy but very credulous to deny your own interest and to declare that others make decisions to back their own interests.

> *How much do I love a proposal of my own?*
> It is extremely easy to cheat yourself and others at the same time. As we evaluate a pleasant thing, we tend to belittle its risks and costs, and simultaneously exaggerate its benefits. Repulsive things distract us the other way. The stronger we are against something, the more we will find points for criticism.

Where are the differing opinions?
If a management team is about to make a quick decision in consensus, at least one of the members ought to challenge options. When differing opinions are missed this is a warning sign.

Where are the options?
Good decision-making contains evaluation of alternatives. However, both individuals and groups tend to build a single credible sounding hypothesis and then they search for facts that support it. If the management team gets a „finalised‰proposal, it is advisable to ask the presenter: Which options did you consider? At which stage did you abandon them? Why? Thus, it is good practice to require at least a couple of options and a clarification of their advantages and disadvantages for the primary proposal.

Where do the figures come from?
Critical analysis of essential figures behind the proposal helps us to detect a potential anchoring bias. We have to ask: which of these figures are actual figures, which are estimates?

Do you see a halo effect?
This phenomenon makes us see a story as being more logical and credible than it really is. We tend to put a „halo‰on a person who is considered as out-standing, and that is why s/he only seldom has to deal with tricky questions. People do not want to overdo their importance or to take the risk of revealing their own stupidity. Better to keep quiet.

Where is the proposal if placed in the continuum of cautious – courageous?
If the decisions are systematically on the safe side, the organization ends up under performing. There is no creativity or ambition and attention is on securing the business. If the decisions are on the contrary, constantly even reckless, the consequences may be irreversible. When considering a proposal, it is good to keep in mind the level of caution or courage that goes with it.

TRY THIS: Wireframe model for decision-making (applied, Drucker 1967)

1. Target of the decision

   - Common agreement of the core of the decision: What is this decision about? Which problem will we solve with this decision?

2. Decision options

   - Recognize alternative decisions: Which options do we have?

3. Analysis of impacts

   - Consider the impacts and consequences of the decision: Different options?

---

4. Decision

   • Make the right decision: Whom and what does the chosen decision primarily support? Which value does it strengthen? But note: the right decision is seldom the most pleasant.

5. Communicating the decision

   • Take care in informing key persons: Who needs to know about this decision? How do we ensure that the required information reaches the right places?

6. Succeeding in decisions

   • Stop in due time to evaluate your decisions: How did we succeed with our decisions? What do we learn from our decisions and their impacts?

New energy to the meetings

It starts with priming your thinking, but successful management team meetings demand structures and practices that support brain performance. Predictability supports effectiveness, and therefore the contents and rhythm of meetings should be logical. You might want to divide the meetings into, for example, „standard‰ and „theme‰meetings. The rhythm is connected to the annual cycle of strategy process and other management processes. Also all the management forums on various levels need to be synchronized with each other, so that the processing does not get stuck at the annoying statement „it has not yet been dealt with at the lower/ higher level before it comes to us‰

Best practices of theme meetings

Issues that require more interpretation and conversation should be placed in theme meetings. Typical themes are

• Strategic investments
• Customer accounts
• Human resources development
• Technology development
• Evaluation of profit and loss, and profitability
• Understanding the business environment
• Internal efficiency and cooperation in the management team

Theme meetings may have external opening speakers and the duration is longer than a standard meeting, in general from a half to a whole day. In general the meeting should not be held in the familiar meeting room. The person responsible for the theme topic takes care of the preparation of the meeting. The chair or facilitator of the theme meeting is typically somebody else than the chair of standard meetings.

Developing standard meetings

Standard meetings give configuration to daily operations and decision-making. A systematic structure will steer the course of the meeting. The agenda of standard meeting is divided into three natural phases: before, during and after the meeting. Next we present a list of the required activities in the form of an exercise.

DEVELOP: Programme for developing meeting practices

Before the meeting

1. Distribution of the agenda
2. Quality of the agenda
3. Personal preparation
4. Advance materials and resolution proposals

At the meeting

5. Schedules
6. Discussion
7. Decision-making
8. Focus

After the meeting

9. Information
10. Execution
11. Follow-up
12. Unity
13. Managing the management team information

1. Evaluate the AS IS state of management team meetings in each of these 13 items with school grades, each member separately.
2. State a TO BE level of management team meetings in each item, each member separately.
3. Explore together: where do you find the biggest GAPS between as is and to be, and select two or three items for further development.
4. Develop together or in pairs each item: concrete actions, new house rules and specified principles.
5. Finally, make a common decision in your normal way: what, who, when, follow-up etc . . .

Table 5.1 Example – a management team in the finance sector made a list of actions.

Stage	Action	House rules, norms, operation models, argumentation
BEFORE THE MEETING	Distribution of agenda	• CEO responsible for compiling, to participants 2–4 days in advance, additions taken in advance, decision items at least 2 days in advance.
	Quality of agenda	• Items must have significant connection to 1) strategy or 2) development or 3) joint future.
	Personal preparation	• Everyone familiarizes themselves with issues and material in order to be able to participate in forming a joint opinion.
	Materials and proposals	• Sufficient background material so everyone is able to form an opinion.
AT THE MEETING	Schedules	• Opening on time as agreed, stating estimate of required time for each item. • Closing: commitment to joint decisions and no more goofing around. • Respect for joint time, on full steam together!
	Discussion	• Chair acting equitably. • Everyone͡s duty to participate, influence and give positive feedback. • Right to present own opinion, and duty to listen to others and to question in a positive way.
	Decision-making	• Clear recording of decisions: who, what, when and follow-up. • Every decision is public, unless decided otherwise.
	Focus	• Separate items: reporting/monitoring or planning? • Everyone takes care of holding on track.

(*Continued*)

Table 5.1 (Continued)

STAGE	ACTION	House rules, norms, operation models, argumentation
AFTER THE MEETING	Communication	• All decisions are published as standard, unless decided otherwise. • Communication always connected to strategy.
	Execution	• No compromising of decisions, execution as decided at the meeting.
	Follow-up	• Follow-up list of decisions, which is checked at every meeting. • Decision removed from the list only as completed fully. • Concerning decisions only deviations of implementation are reported.
	Unity	• Joint message is absolute as regards loyalty and unity. • We show capability to make decisions and determination of execution. • We act as examples of good leadership. • We set our goals farsightedly and realistically, and we follow up their implementation.
	MT Information	All information in intranet in joint folder, no mailing with attachments, nothing saved in own computers.

Refreshing postures

At the beginning of this chapter, we noted that thinking could be primed even in rather crooked ways. On the other hand, the brain can be primed in many familiar ways to work more efficiently. A sedentary management team has to remember that movement has an amazing impact on the healthy brain. Here are some of the discoveries, which also apply to the activities of not-so-sporty people.

Levitin (2006):

- Synchronizing your body movement to music causes pleasure.
- Synchronizing to the rhythm of another person promotes social interaction.

Saarikallio (2010):

- Positive emotions are connected to a standing position and a stretched body.
- Fast and wide movements are connected to joy, enthusiasm and hate.
- Positivity increases gestures and head movement.

Brinol and Petty (2003):

- Nodding head promotes acceptance of a message, shaking head promotes rejecting a message.

What could these mean to your meeting practices?

TRY OUT: "Postures"

Guide your management team

- to stand up and handle a problem standing at a flipboard.
- to describe the situation with wide hand movements (like „temperamental Latinos‰ to show how high or wide the goal is etc.
- to nod by asking the team repeatedly to show you that they are following you.

Problem solving changes surprisingly. This is worth trying!

DO IT OTHER WAY: Preparing on your own

Donât show your PowerPoint presentation to your colleagues but share it in printed handouts. Give them 5–10 minutes to study it (or approximately the same time as you would have used for presenting it quickly). After that you can start immediately with questions and ideas that the presentation has provoked. And then to the decision.

A management team in finance used to call in external experts to make introductory statements and give topical reviews at their meetings. These speeches took a significant part of the time in the meeting agenda. As the meetings extended regularly to 4 or 5 hours, an external coach proposed a radical change to that practice. They ended up with a new presentation culture:

- *The presenter may use of 1–2 slides, where the first one is a summary of the presentation and the second the question about which he or she wants to get comments from the management team.*
- *Slides and potential background material must be sent to the management team at least one day prior to the meeting.*
- *The agreed time limit is kept strictly. If the presentation goes overtime it is interrupted. It is important to learn to keep the presentation focused on substance.*
- *The management team always chooses a person who is in charge of making sure before the meeting that each presenter knows how to act according to common principles.*

THINK ABOUT THIS: Structures of meeting

Edgar Schein, the guru of organizational culture, says that structures create behaviour. What kind of behaviour does our meeting structure create? How should we behave? What kind of structures would create the desired behaviour? What kind of structures would create joyful collaboration?

6   Success metrics in the cockpit

GOAL ITCH

Symptoms: Blurred sense of reality, even blindness

Goal itch is roughly an opposite phenomenon to that earlier described as *management team vertigo*. High in a panoramic location it is easy to direct your focus onto a goal far away. At the same time, attention is drawn to the fact that, seen from a high position, the progress down there seems annoyingly slow. This is similar to standing in an observation tower and reviewing the progress of the work only from a distance. There you can see the whole picture, but at the same time, you wait more and more impatiently for the slow changes in the big picture.

  Goal itch weakens the ability in the management team to see human beings and their activities that take them towards the goal. Bad *goal itch* causes a blurred sense of reality and cold behaviour toward subordinates. These commonly lead to a diagnosis of *malignant leadership* that may develop into *human blindness*. Chronic *goal itch* is always dangerous for collaboration and long term success.

Care instructions in Appendix 2: ÂSelf care guide for management teamsÊ

Metrics connected to strategy

The launch pad of the management team is now only missing the finish. When the management team has defined its mission and vision, as well as created strategic guidelines and adjusted the decision-making body, only the discussion related to success metrics is left. Measurement and its methods add firmness to the launch pad, as the actual journey begins. How does the Stellar Team take advantage of the opportunities associated with measurement?

  It is a well-known fact that measurement inevitably affects action, but nevertheless, you often measure what is easiest to measure. In many management teams measurement is connected to beliefs. We strive for excessive accuracy, qualitative measurements are disparaged and mathematical averages are trusted disproportionately.

In management teams the focus is traditionally on financial indicators, because the goal of management is profit. There are risks with financial meters in any case. They can guide us towards short-term thinking and planning, as well as to partial optimization. If the focus is too much on monetary indicators, they begin to overshadow non-monetary based indicators that evaluate, for example, customer satisfaction, skills, and success in change agility. Economic indicators often show the results of finished operations and that is why they serve as information for decision-making only from one level. More is needed.

Well-formed metrics are always connected to strategy. No matter which metrics are used, the ultimate starting point is the guidelines, which most credibly will lead to the intended goal. Goal setting in the management team goes traditionally according to the following formula.

1. Define a common goal that is sufficiently explicit and clear. In a business enterprise it is, of course, essential also to the success of the business, and it is linked in one way or another to the creation of economic value.
2. Create a common understanding of a background theory, or at least of the variables that contribute to the achievement of that goal. In financial metrics, the most common variables are for example related to turnover, costs, investments, operating profit, cash flow or return on investment. The list could, of course, continue with non-fiscal variables; for example customer loyalty, customer satisfaction, and even aspects of product quality. A simple example of background thinking is that loyal customers contribute to the value creation of the company.
3. Define the actions and activities to be taken in order to achieve the desired goals, i.e. create a link between the goals and the metrics. So, for example, it would be good to understand the factors that generate and promote customer loyalty. One of the best suppositions could be, for example, a low rate of staff changes in customer service.

This is how the definition of goals and the construction of their success metrics proceed. This is a functioning method, which, as such, serves business management. However, the above template still falls short of the Stellar Team approach.

A Stellar Team always sets goals on two levels. In the highest management team, traditional goal setting is linked naturally to the achievement of the goals of the entire organization. As the management team is accountable to the board of directors, the management team tries to do all in its power to achieve the goals and to ensure that the board is happy. In the case of a unit or department management team, the economic performance indicators have been given from the „top‰ They measure the success of the management team and the whole unit at the same time.

In addition to this very typical measurement, which is based on traditional goal setting, the Stellar Team also measures success on levels which are based on the idea of Primary and Secondary Goals.

Primary and secondary success metrics

The Stellar Team has now defined the company's mission, vision and strategy, and has also done the same for the management team itself. The Stellar Team has created together an inspiring picture of the future, which focuses on the accomplishments of the management team and on how its action appears when the vision is achieved. In addition, common conversations have produced an understanding of how the team believes it will cross the finishing line.

Secondary success indicators focus on accomplishments that the management team wants to achieve within a certain time frame. The secondary metrics of the Stellar Management Team relate to each of its members. Management team level secondary metrics may include, for instance, the creation of systematics for meeting practices, activities to activate external stakeholders or the improvement of indicators concerning 180/360 feedback for management team members or evaluations of the whole management team.

The management team of a trading company decided at the beginning of their development process to do a Systemic Leadership Pulse[1] evaluation, where they wanted in particular, to get an idea of the management team's image in different parts of the organization. The survey questions explored this image and they produced both numeric and qualitative material. As the feedback in this case was critical throughout, the management team chose a few common variables for their development areas and goals.

The following two challenges were prioritized:

1. Management team communication.
2. Coherent functioning of the management team members according to joint guidelines.

According to the survey, the averages of responses in both items were well below 3 on a scale of 1 to 5, so the target level was set moderately at 3.5. In addition, they decided to focus on the impression, which was transmitted in the open feedback: the management team was considered a secret society. They decided to repeat the survey next year, so they had a discussion of the strategic choices, which would support them in achieving their Secondary Goal. The summary of the discussion showed the following:

1. Each management team meeting should end with a discussion of the issues that each member undertakes to communicate in his/her own meetings within a week.

2.   *The minutes of the management team meeting will be simplified and, in accordance with the agreed principles, the minutes must be available for all in the companyÊ IntraWeb one day after the meeting.*

3.   *The management team will divide into so-called sparring pairs. Each member has his own sparring partner, who will visit the meetings of the colleague in order to (a) get acquainted with the mode of operation and (b) to harmonize practices in accordance with the agreed guidelines. Sparring pairs will always work six weeks at a time, during which time each pair will create their own practice for goal oriented operation. After that there will be a joint feedback discussion at the level of the whole management team and then the next partner gets the „treatment‰ This way, each member will become familiar with all the five colleagues in the next few months.*

Priorities regarding measurement of Primary Goals

A Stellar Team sets the Primary Goals also for their own actions. As the following chapter will deal with Primary Goals in more detail, we present here only the essential aspects linked to measurement. The key is to focus your attention on how the team works as a collective team. Secondary Goals, in turn, direct your attention onto **what** the management team wants to accomplish. In Primary Goals the attention is correspondingly on **how** the members act and interact with each other.

The aspects of Primary Goals may be related to mutual feedback practices, conscious utilization of diversity or to exercises on how to cope with conflict situations.

After their discussion, the management team in the previous story ended with the following statements on Primary Goals and on necessary actions:

1.   *Open feedback culture*
     We will learn to give feedback – both constructive/developmental and positive/supporting. After each meeting we will use about five minutes for common reflection and feedback on the accomplishments of the meeting.

2.   *Management team meetings will go to the top of our priority list*
     We invest in good preparation prior to the meeting and we will learn how to indicate that a joint meeting is important. Preparations will be done primarily in working groups, and in this way, we will learn how to cooperate between the meetings. Meetings will begin at the agreed time, and if someone is late, he/she will offer coffee and pastries to the entire team at the next meeting. There will be discussion after every presentation at the meetings, and everyone is expected to express his/her opinion or pose a good question. There will be no silent members

any more in our meetings. We will learn to discuss and include in our comments elements, which will involve challenge and broaden the perspective.

Note

1 *Systemic Leadership Pulse* is a survey tool for developing management teams, based on the Stellar Team frame of reference and evaluations of the management team members. Systemic Leadership Pulse is developed and owned by BoMentis Oy. www.bomentis.fi

7 Strengthening the launch pad

CULTURE ABSCESS

Symptoms: Odour nuisances and blaming

Culture abscess is not actually a management team disease, but the management team is often the source of the disease and its most powerful transmitter. In a management team that is polluted by *culture abscess*, you hear often the argument: the management team would create success, but we have this kind of culture and that kind of people. Many of the organization researchers have the opinion that everything drains downwards in an organization. Therefore, the management affects the culture more than employees. At worst, it is not even appropriate to talk about draining the *culture abscess*, which means the organization is blessed with „*long live the sacred cows%*culture.

A remarkable diagnosis creator and leadership professional Arto Hiltunen has said the management in Finland has learned to live with their problems. Hiltunen means that companies continue despite the problems – and without solving the problems! In Hiltunen͂s opinion a typical management team is like a County Council: the delegates have designated places, where they sit holding noses high. The real decisions are made elsewhere – and the same is true also of many top-level management teams. According to legislation and corporate by-laws, in most cases, a body called management team simply does not exist. Regardless of where the management team is in the organization chart, it can be said that, in practice, nearly every management team leader could make all the decisions alone. And that even happens very often, which is one of the primary reasons of *culture abscess*. So the pus drains.

Care instructions in Appendix 2: ÅSelf care guide for management teamsÊ

Related to Secondary Goals there are five elements of the launch pad that mould the management team into a functional unit. This will not yet carry us to the stars but by investing in these aspects the flight altitude can be increased significantly. The launch pad gets still another different kind of solidity, when we leave mathematical calculations and look at the Secondary Goals from particular perspectives. In the review are coincidences and successes, which at best will provide the spark for inspiration and promote a culture of enthusiasm.

Coincidence generates different results than control

Where is the focus of concentration in management teams? It is obvious at meetings. The world is getting more complex, the number of options and options for options increase. We are approaching a system which is so complicated that the capacity of one single director or one management team will not be enough for praiseworthy management.

Is there a danger that people will start to function without management – and make better solutions with swarm intelligence in such complex systems? Or will the contemporary quest for standardization gain domination? The standardization of processes has a clear objective: accidental coincidence must be prevented by control. We do know, however, that a number of great inventions in history were born by chance.

It seems that at least Finnish management and management teams have a strong need for control.

In 2013 HRM Partners Oy, a Finnish consulting company, interviewed 70 management teams in Finland. The local business newspaper, Kauppalehti, reported on their webpage the following summary:

- *People that are selected for management teams are fact and numeric oriented. In management teams their representation was 77% but in the control group 59%.*
- *There are 1.9 times more „organizers%in management teams than elsewhere who focus on systematic administration and control. In addition to this, there are even 2.4 times more „managers%focusing on planning than in the control group.*
- *The number of people who are people oriented by nature, is in management teams only 23%, but in the control group 41%.*

The conclusion of this report is that Finnish management teams are leaders for stable times, which includes systematic control and minor improvement. In a growth company we have to look for new opportunities bravely, we must make experiments and mistakes – but obviously we lack the appropriate mentality for that.

A different kind of success

A number of analysts have over the years tried to find an irrefutable model for successful business. Daniel Kahneman, Nobel Prize winner in Economics, thinks that the task is absolutely impossible, because good luck is involved in the success of even the best companies. Kahneman has a formula for success which deviates from the average: „success = talent + luck‰At the end of luck you return back to the average.

For example, the top companies, which were analysed in the classic business books *Built to Last* and *In Search of Excellence*, dropped back to standard level after the analysis. Similarly, in Finland, it seems that the recovery of „*The Export Award of the President of the Republic‰*may drive a success story before long even to bankruptcy.

Chaos is full of coincidences. This is a good link to another favourite formula of Kahneman: „great success = a little more talent + a lot of luck‰However, you cannot encounter „A lot of luck‰by chance, but in the words of Louis Pasteur, chance favours the **prepared** mind. In other words, you may need „a little more talent‰But how can a management team adequately respond and dare to build new structures and practices that will be **preparations** for being favoured by „a lot of luck‰

WAKE UP! CHANGE THE OLD CHAPS IN THE MANAGEMENT TEAM TO YOUNGER GUYS!

– No, not really, we even have another, less enjoyable method to renew your management team: you *have* to start using the neuroplasticity of the brain. That means a strong effort on personal renewal. And on the cultivation of new thinking. Investing in using critical Deep Analysis instead of Hasty Intuition. Acquiring „a little more talent‰No wonder that many directors say they are too old to change themselves! Professor and management researcher David Clutterbuck puts it in other words: many directors are too old to act as directors!

Chance will favour the conscious developer

People operate mostly according to their routines. We use practices that are automatized, and which we have learned a long time ago. The routines are easy, comfortable and energy saving. The transition to a new and, perhaps, a better model requires effort and conscious development. It also includes the risk that the effort may be useless; the new model may not meet our expectations. Therefore, development demands incredible courage to grab onto the new and to deal with frightening, unpleasant things.

Conscious development of conscious activity demands commitment to new, Stellar Team-like dimensions.

A management team in the wholesale trade recognized three important things at the beginning of their development process:

1. *We are willing to endure hard effort*
    We know that development requires continuing perseverance and effort. It means questioning our own practices and thoughts for each one of us. It is uncomfortable, difficult and even painfully demanding, but we know that birth and pain go hand in hand.

2. *We observe intuitions, emotions and energies*
    We know how we are directed automatically by intuition. We are aware that emotions tune our thinking. We help each other to observe differences between intuitive and reflective thinking.
    We are energetic leaders and we know our impatience is connected to high energy. We adjust our energy and we will not let it lead us to actions that are too quick and that may appear unpredictable to the others.

3. *We will develop the control of our minds*
    We practice mindfulness skills: regulation of energy and stress level, focusing on work and on the exclusion of disruption. By developing mindfulness skills we reduce automatic control. We are also able to prioritize our time to essential management tasks.

Coincidences as a new management team focus

A renewing and learning management team thirsts for new challenges and new successes. Earlier in this chapter, it was hinted that many good things happen by chance. If so, what if the new challenge for your management team would be to create favourable environments and situations for a growing number of new, positive coincidences? But how do you differentiate between positive and negative coincidence? A clear strategy simplifies this in business. A positive coincidence supports the strategy, a negative one does not. Therefore, the management must ensure that the organization has a strategy, which is clear and, above all, that everybody knows it.

OPPORTUNITIES: Strategic coincidences in your management team

What would „coincidence as management team focus‰ mean in our practices? How do we create a favourable environment for positive coincidences? How do we ensure that everybody recognizes as many as possible? How do we implement the formula „great success = a little more talent + a lot of luck‰

Constant or repeated renewal?

If you do something continuously without sufficient breaks, it normally causes a state of nervous system that is called in its mildest form tiredness. Tiredness is not good for learning or renewal, but for those purposes it is good to model physical training. This is a combination of series of movements and then a break and repeating the movements again etc. So it is repetition, not continuing.

A management team acting professionally must repeatedly have the energy and ability to question their own understanding and ways of acting. Again and again. Repetition becomes easier as the team and each of its members consciously acquire new and wider approaches.

> WAKE UP! A MANAGEMENT TEAM THAT LIVES IN RENEWAL, ENDEAVOURS TOWARDS BUSINESS OPERATIONS THAT NOBODY ELSE HAS DONE BEFORE.

If renewal is obvious so the management team will be able to answer this: What new thing can we test now – meaning immediately – even though we maybe do not know if it will work? What is the talent in our success formula where we can add a little luck?

PREPARE: Before the meeting

As chair of the management team or presenter of a single item you can consider these before your meeting:

- What is the best input that each participant can put into each item?
- How do you assist them to do so?
- What kind of management culture, collaboration culture and company culture will our next meeting support?

Success focused operation

Discussing problems is normal in management teams. Unexpected issues just appear on agendas and they require joint decision-making and response. We have been cultivating the word „problem%so much, that in the last few years we have desired to get rid of that word. We do not talk of problems any more, they are challenges.

The word „challenge%gave the impression, at least initially, of being a grade softer and, in general, people were tricked into working a little more eagerly. On the other hand, if there was a problem, you needed to find a solution. The need for a solution did not change, even if the word had changed. Instead of focusing on the selection of the right word, the perspective as regards brain function is better for stimulating the thoughts.

We have a unique skill to build problems in our mind. The production of problems is inborn in our brain connections. A problem is, in principle, a negatively coloured viewpoint, but it has always a positive intention. Fortunately, it is never too late to modify thinking. That̂s why it is good practice to let a solution pop up. You have probably noticed that your missing keys know how to find you. The questions are what, who, how – not why. You have to face the problems and then let „the common brain‰of the management team to find a solution.

PROBLEM: Road to solution

1. Choose a problem that needs a successful solution.
2. When has that problem been ÂbetterÊ what was it like when it did not cause so much harm?
3. What can you do to make that happen more often?
4. What will people then notice about you and the situation?
5. How do you know that the problem is solved successfully?
6. What is now your first step on the road to a solution?

How should this be?

A success focused solution to the problem is based on emotions, needs and values in the present state. The most important thing is to know how they should be taken into account in the future. The key to that direction is the success focused solution model, in which the investment of energy and time is guided according to the following percentages:

- 70% – How do we describe our successful solution, good result, fulfilled objective? What is that success like in detail? What does it look like, how do people talk about it, how does it feel, taste, smell?
- 20% – What elements do we already have in place for the existence of that success, what resources, skills and attitude do we have for it? What do we already have and what else is needed?
- 10% – What shall we do now, how do we begin, what is our action plan? How do we proceed towards success?

Solely analysing a problem or a negative phenomenon can lead to the obsessive seeking of a solution that causes anxiety and feelings of inadequacy, threat and fear. Negative emotions weaken the broad-based use of the brain, which is in practice, efficient and analytical thinking of Deep Analysis. The success focused model directs the attention to a successful solution and it creates, instead of negative emotions, enthusiasm, joy, self-efficacy, and the satisfaction of accomplishment.

A management team in the process industry had concluded that it felt absurd to ask „How should this be?‰when the damage had occurred. In their case, an IT system failure caused a large amount of manual work. Now they were just keen to analyse why the accident took place. An interesting version of the success focused question was generated, as the management team first thought of its own auto-reply: „This should be so that the damage would not have occurred‰Then they could proceed on a success focused path, as they stated, that damages must be prevented and thus they asked: „What will prevent future damages?‰This steered in a natural way forwards to the statement: „In the future this shall be so, that the. . . ‰

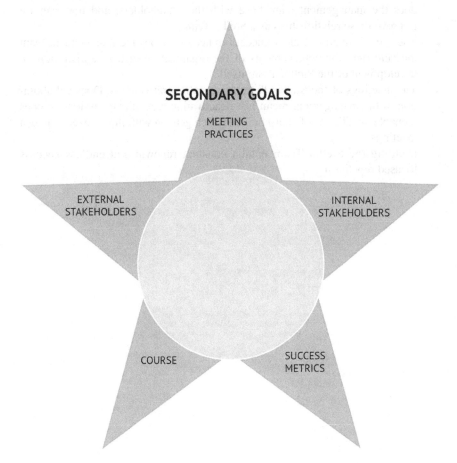

Figure PS.II Star: Secondary Goals describe what a Stellar Team does in collaboration and why it cooperates

Core of Part II: Secondary Goals as launch pad

In this book we are taking a metaphoric journey to the stars, in other words we are going to develop the management team into a Stellar Team that will raise its operations to a new level of results. In Part II we have seen the Secondary Goals of the management team as being a launch pad for our development journey.

- The Stellar Team has a mission and a vision of its own. Why does this team exist and what kind of a Stellar Team do we want to become? What is our guiding star?
- The Stellar Team realizes it is living in a world of relationships. Who are our most important external and internal stakeholders? What kind of relationships

does the management team have with the stakeholders, and how can we improve those relationships as a Stellar Team?

- The Stellar Team has clear success indicators. Does the management team measure only the achievements of the organization or do we also monitor development of the Stellar Team itself?
- The meetings of the Stellar Team serve collaborative ends. Does collaboration in the management mean just deactivating rear-mirror sessions or does it enable an alliance of sharp brains, which gets on with things even between meetings?
- Building the Stellar Team entails constant renewal and endless success focused repetition.

Part III

Attraction of Primary Goals

Figure PIII.1 Primary Goals: Primary Goals describe how the Stellar Team acts to obtain the best possible results in collaboration

8 Commitment is the core of guiding star

SACRED COW DISEASE

Symptoms: Avoidance of broaching issues and silent sprouting of culture abscesses

Sacred cow disease has its breeding ground in a management team whose greatest strength is that it has learned to live with its problems. This team is a kind of group of naked emperors, who have learned not to talk about their embarrassing lack of clothing. This type of conscious living in a common lie will have an effect at an unconscious level by paralysing trust and degenerating commitment. In the case of this disease, it is good to recall its cultural ties. It is well known that the cow is a sacred animal in India and it is treated as it deserves. Cows are allowed to pass and lie down anywhere, and it really seems that Indians do not even see them. The invisible things within a management team with *sacred cow disease* are visible to everybody else but the disease lulls us into believing that those things are not supposed to be seen. It is easy to come up with a list of sacred cows: abuse, lying, injustice, under-achievement, alcoholism, breach of promise, incompetence, inadequate qualification, etc.

Care instructions in Appendix 2: ẪSelf care guide for management teamsÊ

There are two types of commitment within ourselves

Commitment is seen as a quality of an ideal employee. The higher position an employee has, the more important commitment is regarded. Lack of commitment is visible in many actions and the most common lies in working life concern commitment. Let us study how commitment comes about and how it is expressed in a management team.

There are many ways in which a person can be divided into two complementary parts. We have already dealt with the two systems of thinking: Hasty Intuition and Deep Analysis. Hasty Intuition leads us, for example, to commit to familiar things and nice guys. Of course, a new development project cannot be a familiar thing, but Hasty Intuition rapidly identifies some of the same familiar features as in certain earlier projects. In the same way „the nice guys‰ can be quite new acquaintances, but, for example, there may be memories from an earlier presentation, or from the persons former job, previous position and the impression of having a sturdy chin. Thus, Hasty Intuition can quickly produce an evaluation of „nice guy‰ or similarly, quickly lead us to watch out for commitment, if those previous memories tend to raise doubts or a threat.

Deep Analysis builds commitment through slow thinking. I can search for justifiable arguments for the idea which is produced by Hasty Intuition. You can stop and steer slow thinking for example with the following questions:

- What importance do I get from this?
- What importance do the other parties get?
- What new and important things does this generate?
- What existing and important things does this protect?

Two types of egoism – the right and the wrong one?

An individuals egoism emphasizes the self. Egoism can be considered from two perspectives. From the perspective of moral philosophy, ethical egoism requires that a man should act in accordance with his own interests. In psychology, the theory of egoism explains human activity through natural egoism. Should the management team combine ethical and psychological egoism? What would that kind of egoism produce as an engine of action?

Own interest is the most important guiding principle in operating a company. Own interest guides towards the creation of long-term profits. Maximizing the interests of the company and shareholders requires in the long term that the company also treat all stakeholders in a just manner. This self-interest in business might justly be called egoism.

The egoism of an individual is easily recognized and it is very common. It occurs between members of the management team in competition for attention, stage time and resources. It seeks its own immediate advantage; it is partial optimization and short-term thinking. It is displayed as vanity and selfish behaviour. Such egoism is easily classified as „wrong‰ but is there a „right‰ egoism?

According to psychological egoism, seeking our own interest motivates us the most in any case. „What do I get?‰ is a natural question, the purpose of which is to steer us to direct towards benefit or indirect benefit. In the latter case direct benefit will guide us to any other party that has a relevant meaning for us.

From the ninth century we can find a very apt description of human selfishness. We only needed to add the four emboldened words to the writing of Mohammed Ibn Al-Jahm Al-Barmaki:

> **In the management team** „*no one deserves thanks from another about something he has done for him or goodness he has done, he is either willing to get a reward from God, therefore he wanted to serve himself, or he wanted to get a reward from people, therefore, he has done that to get profit for himself, or to be mentioned and praised by people, therefore, to it is also for himself, or due to his mercy and tenderheartedness, so he has simply done that goodness to pacify these feelings and treat himself‰*
>
> (Source and translation Wikipedia)

The processing of material and immaterial values requires ethical egoism. Profit and ownership have been decisive factors in the emergence of the market economy. The pursuit of efficiency has launched a variety of business activities, and now we have all the best available, both material and cultural; food, heat and medicines as well as smart phones and entertainment channels.

Me, myself and I, and once more me. The emphasis on oneself and maximizing one's own interests is not ethical egoism. If players acting out of own personal interest dominate, at the expense of the interest of company or colleague, it is pointless to even fantasize about building a Stellar Team. The morality of the team is eroded and „wrong behaviour‰will begin to spread.

The counter power to the erosion of the morality is ethical egoism, which directs the quest for profit to the benefit of the company, or at least to the common interest of the management team. We need to commit ourselves to more than the optimization of personal incentives. When a common goal and, working together gets more space, commitment to the common can grow. A Stellar Team derives its oxygen from common commitment. Without this flame cooperation fades away and the team no longer produces a warm atmosphere and does not generate any good for its members. An atmosphere of personal interests strengthens sullenness and protection of status.

P. Lencioni, a developer of leadership and management teams, crystallizes the meaning of commitment:

> „The ultimate dysfunction of a team is the tendency of members to care about something other than the collective goals of the group.‰
>
> (Lencioni 2002)

The most important erosive element of the potential in the management team is that members are not committed to their common objective. In the „test‰in Table 8.1 we explore first the connection between egoism and values, in other words, we will see how a positive event implements your values. In the second part we try to orientate ourselves through egoism and values towards ethical egoism, i.e. we will look at how you can promote the common good through your values.

Table 8.1 WIFM Tests.

WIFM Test 1	WIFM Test 2
1. Name some positive event in your past life.	1. Select a positive event where your management team participated.
2. Who was present at that event?	2. What importance did you get for yourself from that? What did the management team get? What did your organization get?
3. What made that event positive?	3. Select another event: What importance did you get from that for yourself? What did the management team get? What did your organisation get?
4. What was the most important thing for you in that event?	4. Being an ethical egoist, how would you promote the important things you found in previous questions?
5. What was important to you that the event gave to the other participants?	

TEST: Test yourself with WIFM Tests!

A reward system steers

Money and different types of economic benefits affect the behaviour of individuals, although this is not always admitted. They are not necessarily motivating factors, but they will certainly affect each and everyone, at least as background variables. We know from motivation studies that actual moving forces spring from completely other sources – from passion, significance of an experience and from the atmosphere of a variety of actions, alone or together with others. Financial incentives do not appear in the top positions of those lists of motivators.

WAKE UP! IF THERE ARE MANAGEMENT TEAM MEMBERS WHO ARE LED BY INDIVIDUAL AND FINANCIAL GOALS, THEIR COMMITMENT IN THE FIRST PLACE IS TO PROMOTE THEIR INDIVIDUAL AND FINANCIAL AMBITIONS.

Where are the common objectives of the management team and the common incentives? Where are those organizations and management teams who are steered more by a common goal than by objectives of individual actions? Fortunately, the management team is able to change the situation and to develop measurable goals that lead towards their guiding star. The Stellar Team will succeed when also the common success indicators support commitment (see Chapter 6, „Success metrics in the cockpit%

Is collective responsibility a collective mistake?

Commitment is closely linked to responsibility. We talk about individual and collective responsibility. Both of them are official goals in many management teams. Solidarity is very noble, but many people claim, based on their experience, that in an awkward situation, collective responsibility is going to be no one's responsibility.

Taking common responsibility too irresponsibly often causes escape from common responsibility. Hasty Intuition is the cause of repentance. Let us assume that the next question comes up in the management team:

–   This is an investment proposal, is this worth investing in?

Hasty Intuition tries to produce an answer based on information available, but if there is no information, it may replace the original, complicated question with an easier one:

–   What are the options for an investment?
–   How much do we have in assets now?
–   Has our competitor made a similar investment?
    (Or even: – I think I don't know so much about this investment that I can take any responsibility, but does it look like the others know better?)

I easily get an answer to my „wrong‰ question and next, the answer begins to influence the team. Group pressure increases and a need to show off arises. Stupidity starts to converge and form an opinion with growing enthusiasm and finally, the team accepts the investment proposal.

Unfortunately there is limitless evidence of this phenomenon, called confirmation bias, both in politics and business. A prime example of this is the conversation in the US government of the Japanese threat just before the attack on Pearl Harbour. (They came to the conclusion that the Japanese would not attack.)

9 Trust creates energy

POWER SCABIES

Symptoms: Extremes of behaviour and an infected atmosphere

Power scabies is a very annoying disease in management teams at all levels. The occurrence of the disease always has very negative effects on confidence. *Power scabies* is identified by the behaviour of individual members of management teams. Specific features of the disease include the following:

- The need to be honoured and to be treated in an exceptional way. The affected individuals do not wait for their turn, they desire to obtain extra perks and want to be first. They also demand undivided attention. If their wish is neglected, they will be annoyed and irritated, even enraged.
- Glorification or annulment. The patients so affected either immediately idolize or invalidate their discussion partner. They flatter, adore, admire and praise or instead, frown on, offend and humiliate the other. There are no forms of behaviour in between.
- The emphasis is on self. The *power scabies* patient boasts continually. The speech repeats me, myself, and I. At the same time the disease removes the ability to take an interest in others and their words. His/her behaviour tends towards the bored and ignorant, if the patient is not the centre of the discussion.
- An inability to empathise. The most obvious sign of *power scabies* is the lack of ability to accommodate the other person̂s position. Patients are constantly stuck in their own little world and they seek to justify their own experience and their being right – in one way or another.

Care instructions in Appendix 2: ̂Self care guide for management teamŝ

Trust and its reinforcement are at the heart of the Primary Goals for the management team that wants to become a Stellar Team. Sustainable success is generated by investing in the internal confidence in the team. When a management team has the desire to build trust at team level and between all the members of the team, its effects are visible in joint action. All human interaction is related to trust, in one way or another.

Trust is a complex and multidimensional phenomenon. Trust is at the level of an individual:

> The individual̂s willingness to expose oneself to another, believing that the other one acts in line with expectations, without the need for watching or observing.
>
> (Laine 2008: 19)

Management teams are often battlefields for different types of power struggles, and that leaves only random opportunities to expose oneself to others. Lack of confidence does not, however, extinguish collaboration completely. Even a small flame is enough to run through the joint meetings. Of course, then there is no trace of a real Stellar Team, because the shortage of trust effectively drains all energy for reform and development. This is inefficiency and a waste of potential, because the attention is on ensuring onês own position and on controlling the movements of others. How do you create any trust here, in concrete terms?

Trust is worth exploring

The importance of trust always comes up in talks about team development. Straight talking clearly does not help, because the whole concept of trust remains easily just as abstract words without any tangible grip. Based on our own experience, and on some high level thinkers, we have gathered behavioural factors that are seamlessly connected to trust.

Table 9.1 Factors increasing and decreasing trust

Increases trust	*Decreases trust*
Consistency and predictability	Insecurity and disappointments
Reciprocity	Pursuit of own interests and protecting own territory
Sharing information and open communication	Concealing information and spreading rumours
Appreciation and respect. Acknowledgement of know-how and the value of others	Mutual competition and negative understanding of others
Commitment and collective responsibility	Lack of commitment and escaping from responsibility

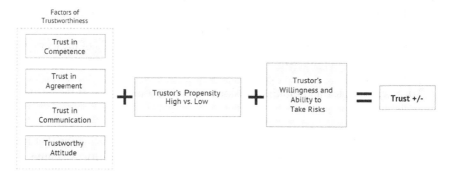

Figure 9.1 Elements of trust

These things are easy to list but concerning interaction they are at the same time important processes and practices. All the factors, which increase confidence, are feasible but they do not come without effort.

We find more understanding of trust from the observations of David Schoorman's research team (Schoorman, Mayer and Davis 1995). The experience of trust is born through four elements: (1) ability, (2) integrity of words and actions, (3) communication style and (4) an attitude of benevolence. The management team has to make all these elements visible.

We have applied these management team observations by crystallizing them into a model in Figure 9.1, which offers an excellent base for evaluation and discussion in the Stellar Team.

Trust in competence is easily detected

If the trustor sees that the other person knows his or her job, there is no reason to worry about the quality of the final result. The trustor can be sure, that the colleague has sufficient knowledge to carry the agreed responsibility. Trust in competence gets stronger. Similarly, suspicion about the inadequacy of the other's ability is easily recognizable. It is apparent, whose competence is not trusted: the person is under suspicion and needs to be controlled. Also the number of delegated tasks decreases if competence is not trusted.

Trust in agreement means integrity

The second trust factor comes from the alignment and integrity of words and deeds. Integrity is at the heart of trust in agreement and it means that action and thoughts are consistent, incorruptible and uncompromisingly honest.

The influence of integrity in building trust is, according to research, highest at the beginning of a collaborative relationship. The better the alignment of words and deeds is, the more this creates trust. Collaboration will be smooth when you know the other party will hold to their promises. If your energy goes on spying and on continuous controlling of agreed actions, trust will fade away.

Communication styles build trust

Now let us look at some communication trust related stereotypes, which serve us with goal oriented new facts for cooperation with different people. People have been distributed into a variety of boxes throughout the ages with more and less scientific tests. Compartmentalization of people creates stereotypes and this is often stifling, because many of us possess qualities from neighbouring compartments.

Stereotypes are needed in developing our thinking. In order to structure thinking from a random „this and that‰level up to a categorizing level, we need first „either/or‰stereotypes. Only then will we be able to expand towards flexible and broad-based „both/and‰thinking. If we want to . . .

All human classifications also serve a great truth: people are different. Some examples of the most common categorizations are: fact oriented – people oriented, extrovert – introvert, dominant – adaptive and thinking – sensing.

An effective team builds trust through the „joy of cognitive flow‰The team takes care to promote diversified communication, which offers everyone a chance to find familiar sounding similarity. Thus, you create confidence between different people in the team.

One of the most useful models for treating diversity and development of communication trust is the behavioural style analysis Peili™ from Integro Finland. Peili (Finnish for mirror) focuses on the visible features of behaviour and it divides diversity into four basic types. In building trust each basic type needs to have its own kind of behaviour from the other party. A success-oriented management team should invest in building trust.

Four dimensions of behaviour

The Peili™ analysis presents behaviour styles through two axes, which form a quadrant. The vertical axis represents the orientation of informal vs. formal, while the horizontal axis represents dominant vs. easy-going. Combinations of these properties are called behavioural styles, and they are named Promoting, Supporting, Analysing and Controlling styles. Reports show that each behavioural style is linked to a typical communication style for building trust. The promoting style appreciates open communication style, Supporting appreciates acceptance, Analysing appreciates reliability and Controlling appreciates straightforward communication style. In the following, we present some of the most important features of each communication style, which promote building trust.

Open communication style

A person whose communication style is mostly based on openness, appreciates voluntary sharing of information and the expression of thoughts and emotions.

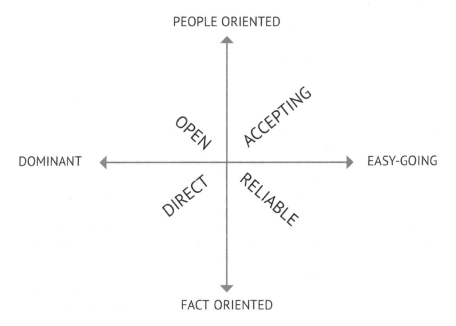

Figure 9.2 Communication styles underlying communication trust

If the responsibility of communication is transferred to others and information is skimped on, distrust sensors begin to react.

DO THIS – share information voluntarily, expressing thoughts and emotions.

- We hold meetings and appointments appropriately, often enough and well enough.
- We communicate to all parties?
- We share all information, we donȄ leave any secrets.
- We share the big picture.
- We discuss emotions, expectations, views and facts connected to the issue.
- We are available and reachable, we give additional information if required.

WATCH OUT – do not transfer communication responsibility to others or conceal information because this will erode the trust of a person who appreciates an open communication style.

- „This must be communicated only by the CEO.‰
- „I cannot tell you about this yet.‰
- „ItȄ better not to talk about this yet.‰

Straightforward communication style

A straightforward communicator says what he or she means and means what he or she says. Straightforward communication is logical and consistent, no matter if the issue is positive or negative. If a person with this style meets fudge, avoidance or beating around the bush, trust will not arise – on the contrary.

DO THIS – be logical in action and communication, both in negative and positive cases.

- We talk about things directly.
- We use appropriate methods for settling disputes.
- We comply with discipline as individuals and in our team.
- We analyse errors sufficiently.
- We find out the expectations.
- We do not conceal our true intentions.
- „I say what I mean and I mean what I say.‰

WATCH OUT – do not fudge and beat around the bush or flatter, because it erodes the trust of a person who appreciates a straightforward communication style.

- „I donÊt know how to put it . . . instead of that I might tell you . . .‰
- „LetÊs not talk about it, weÊd better just leave it.‰
- „You are the smartest guy on this planet and your team is the most efficient in the whole of Europe.‰

Reliable communication style

A representative of the reliable style remains calm and business-like in any situation. Emotions are not really visible because the impact of communication is based on credibility and detailed information. If one starts to exaggerate and to promise too much, or to colour the story without factual evidence, trust in communication will be jeopardised.

DO THIS – stay on the case, be precise, punctual and stay with the facts.

- We define fees and limits on a consistent basis.
- We are committed to decisions.
- We agree that everyone takes responsibility for their own actions.
- We comply with appropriate and sufficient rituals (for example job orientation, greeting, holidays, etc.).
- We will ensure that everyone in the team acts in line with the common objectives.
- We conclude that the team keeps promises and acts according to them, even in relation to persons outside the team.
- „Trust my word.‰

WATCH OUT – do not exaggerate, colour your words or give empty promises, because it will erode the trust of a person who values the reliable communication style.

- „This is the best in the whole world . . .‰

- „This will change your work to relaxation in paradise.‰
- „I will make you a millionaire in 30 days!‰

Accepting communication style

The heart of an accepting communication style is the giving of space to others. This communication style displays a patient attitude to others and is characterized by ample listening. On the other hand, if this person hears judgemental communication and criticism, his/her trust barometer starts to plummet.

DO THIS – give space to other people, listen, be patient and respect diversity.

- We show mutual respect.
- We respect diversity: different ideas, values, opinions, ways of living.
- We change leadership purposefully.
- We participate in and influence decision-making together.
- We listen to each other.
- „To err is human.‰

WATCH OUT – do not criticise others, judge or rule out different views, because it will erode the trust of a person who appreciates an accepting communication style.

- „Your attitude is a problem.‰
- „Pete is a slow and negative colleague.‰
- „You cannot think that way, the fact is . . ‰

People are and will be different. In good cooperation you can see the differences, you understand how they appear, you accept the underlying values, and you take all that into common use.

All the previous ways of building trust emphasise in their own way their own communication style. The better the members of management team take into consideration the different views in their communication, the more they will amass „credits‰in their column of trust in communication.

Did you note: Diversity in opening

At the beginning of this section headed „Communication styles build trust‰ was the very first sentence: „Now letŝ look at some communication trust related stereotypes, which serve us with (1) **goal oriented**, (2) **new** (3) **facts** for (4) **cooperation** with different people.‰

- How could you use diversity and the four perspectives of trust building in a similar way in opening you own speeches and statements?

Trust as regards attitude is perceivable

The last element in building trust is trust in attitude. This is the way the trustor experiences the communication of another person and the justification and motives of his or her actions. If you act benevolently, seeking the common good or good for another, it will create fertile ground for the growth of trust. Similarly, the growth of nascent trust is prevented if the trustor detects signs of „malevolent‰ optimization of own interest and the highlighting of self-importance, often at the expense of the others. A deficit of trust in attitude quickly produces a need to protect yourself and to stay in your own bolthole, because malevolence breaks and destroys. The characteristics of trust as regards attitude come more into play if the team has been more in contact with each other. On our Stellar Teamŝ journey benevolence is superior to evil.

The four elements of building trust can be detected and evaluated in the collaboration of the management team. You can run a quick test for the trust level by evaluating the trust you direct towards each colleague. In the case of a deficit in trust it is particularly important to identify which type of trust sows the seed of mistrust.

Identified factors of mistrust do not just remain as results in individual minds, but a Stellar Team will discuss these and also give fair feedback. The more feedback is shared between the members, the better the chances are to achieve real changes.

We have described above the four levels of building trust: trust in competence, trust in agreement, trust in communication and trust in attitude. They provide important steps for development to a Stellar Team. But what if we are able to build trust together, but personally I do not know how to trust?

Individual tendency to trust

Trust is known to be sensitive and laborious: it is extremely easy to lose but restoring it takes long-term effort. Each of us has a unique tendency to trust, which has been formed over the years and through a variety of experiences and encounters. The more trust has been violated during your life, the more slowly it will grow. Trust does not necessarily arise, even if the other party were to do everything correctly, in accordance with the above-mentioned four factors of trust. The establishment of trust always requires two parties, the trustor and the trustee. Both roles are needed.

The tendency to trust differs individually. A weak tendency to trust and a strongly negative attitude to trust are mostly produced by Hasty Intuition. Hasty Intuition does not lead to trust, but only to hesitation. Even if you add in a strong analysis of the situation from Deep Analysis, the result will be, at best, on the basis of the negative attitude, only suspicion and mistrust.

Similarly, if the tendency to trust is intuitively strong but the analysis of the situation is weak, Hasty Intuition will quickly cause a blind trust. Gullibility develops into a wise trust with considerations from Deep Analysis, which adds an assessment dimension to the strong tendency to trust.

Here are some good questions:

- Developing weak tendency to trust

  - What makes me hesitate? Is there a fact behind that feeling?
  - What would be the worst thing to happen, if I were to trust now?
  - What would happen at its best, if I decided to trust now?

- Developing strong tendency to trust

  - Think about a person that hesitates. What would they focus on?
  - If I were to question or challenge my thinking, what would that mean right now?
  - What is the thing I am not absolutely sure of?

In order to create effective cooperation we need to exercise trust, which means developing our own intuitive tendency to trust. We will ensure considered results if we remember to rely on Deep Analysis.

To trust requires the courage to take risks

In addition to the four general trust factors and the individual tendency to trust, there is still one individual factor that impacts the dynamics of trust: risk taking ability. Trust is always a willingness to take risks. It means an intentional choice that leads to a shift from one's comfort zone towards uncertainty and confusion. Typical questions which go round in your mind are: How will the others react? What would the others think if they knew what I am really thinking?

Considerations of the trustor are a sign that the risk has been identified and observed. When the process advances, there will be two options. Either the person will experience the risk as being too high and will keep his or her mouth shut – or this person will dare to take the risk and choose to be vulnerable. The person says, what he or she thinks. If taking a risk produces the desired result, both trust and the tendency to trust will grow. Of course, it is also possible that the risk materializes into a humiliating disappointment. The risk assessment was not successful and trust building ended up as a failure.

Risk is therefore a function of trust! Without the willingness and ability to take risks, talking about trust will remain hollow. Taking risks requires courage to choose your position and say out loud, what's on your mind. It is talking honestly.

The atmosphere of the Stellar Team is inductive to risk-taking. The members of the team also tolerate frank and honest talk, because it is simultaneously appreciative. It means at the same time: the speaker wants to trust in us.

THINK ABOUT THIS: How much do you trust?

Think about your management team and rate it on a scale of 0 to 100% for each question.

1. How much do you trust this management team?
2. How much do you want to trust?
3. How much do you trust each individual member of the team?
4. How much do you want to trust him or her?
5. How much does this management team trust you?
6. How much do you want them to trust you?
7. How much does each individual member of management team trust you?
8. How much do you want each one to trust you?
   What can you do to increase mutual trust to the desired level? How do you say „I want to trust you all%

Can you accelerate trust formation?

The Chinese say it simply: you cannot grow a seedling by pulling on it. Is there, however, perhaps some accelerated method for building trust? There is the usual belief that successful interaction is always a technique and clever trick of top guys. A super negotiator will always win the deal. A top leader motivates his employees to accomplish the result he has defined. An outstanding therapist cures his patients.

Let us explore the interaction within a management team through that example of psychotherapy because the significance of interaction has been researched most in that discipline. Lots of research has been conducted, because different schools of therapists have argued about the effectiveness and superiority of different forms of therapy. Studies suggest that patients think that the success of therapy depends on three groups of factors, all of which are related to building trust.

1. Relation factors

Carl Rogers, the father of humanistic psychology, found already in the 1950s that the efficacy of the therapy was influenced by

- an unconditioned, positive attention
- accurate empathy
- congruence, authentic adaptation to the patient.

These factors have since then been confirmed on a number of occasions and by many experts. Warmness, acceptance, authenticity and encouragement are also important factors for efficacy. Could we assume that the efficacy of the members in the management team would be amplified if there were observations of relationship, empathy and acceptance connected to collaboration? In that case mutual trust within the management team will develop when each member

- takes into account the personal objectives of the other members in the management team
- accepts other members as human beings
- is sincere and authentic
- adapts his own way of working to that of the team
- collaborates instead of controlling
- takes into account things that are essential for the team

2.   *Hope and expectations*

Particularly in a tough situation people need to have hope for the better and the possibility to set some kind of positive expectations for the future. Trust will emerge as the management team

- develops both a hopeful mind-set and faith in possibilities, without nullifying or neglecting difficulties or consequences at hand
- draws attention to the existing and future opportunities instead of only analysing past problems.

3.   *Methods and techniques*

In the world of therapy, efficiency appears to be connected to the methods used. From the point of view of an ordinary member of a management team, the methods are not very difficult. Indeed, results improve, when the clients strengths are magnified and the treatment seems empathic, appreciative and emphasises the uniqueness of the client. In addition, it must be in harmony with the clients objectives and the concept of change process, and it has to increase hope and a sense of control. Easy methods, which can be used by everyone in the management team!

Sharing dreams is trusting

An efficient management team needs trust between individuals, as it is trust that promotes collaboration. An astonishingly convincing way to build trust is to share dreams.

Martin Luther Kings speech in Washington 1963, „I have a dream‰ is one of the most legendary examples. King shares a strong dream of black and white people being equal Americans, which creates solid trust and unites the audience to support joint action. It is easy for us to trust a person who speaks frankly of his or her ideals, goals and dreams. Of course, the impact of sharing dreams is stronger when those dreams are to some extent similar to the dreams of the audience.

TRY THIS: Dream on

You will create a unique, subtle and strong atmosphere in the management team when you do the following short exercise together. Everyone should first complete alone the following sentences in a couple of minutes.

1. I have a dream that . . .
2. As that dream gets fulfilled . . . (what are the positive consequences?)
3. As that dream gets fulfilled, we will get . . . (consequences to community or environment)
4. This dream is important to me personally because . . .
5. I believe in this dream because . . .
   Then each member reads in turn their own sentences. It takes courage to be honest but it is rewarding. This is worth trying – in any team or group – and then asking what we learned from this.

---

10 Diversity and conflict competence

DIVERSITY INDIGESTION

Symptoms: Heartburn, name-calling, condensed stupidity

Diversity indigestion is very common in all management cultures on this planet. From mildly annoying heartburn and name-calling behind the back, its symptoms range to the worst verbal abuse and even physical aggression. Progressing to *divergence catarrh*, the disease results in team formation only from similar personalities, which is often followed by harmful *condensation of collective irrationality*. Outside the management team it is called more prosaically *group stupidity*.

As an internal management team disorder *diversity indigestion* is very tedious. In particular, within team members, the symptoms seem to begin with differences of temperament or opinion, but the real reason lies in motherŝ milk.

Care instructions in Appendix 2: Âelf care guide for management teamsÊ

The third theme of Primary Goals is related to diversity and the utilization of divergence in the collaboration of the management team. What is the secret of divergence? Why does it feel so frustrating? Divergence presents the seed of conflict. When it begins to become too bothersome, there will be tensions and they will transform into conflicts.

How does a Stellar Team eliminate the accumulating conflicts? Different operating styles bring appropriate dynamics to cooperation in the Stellar Team. At best, they are the sources of common enthusiasm and creativity, where different strengths are in common use.

It is useful to shy away from diversity

Familiarity creates security and constitutes the foundation of social order and cohesion among humans. Unconsciously we end up favouring things that we have experienced in the past. Unfamiliar things evoke appropriate caution or even fear.

> *Robert Zajonc tested two groups of unhatched chicken eggs by playing them two different tones. Thus, the tone number 1 for the egg group number 1 and the tone number 2 for the egg group number 2. After hatching, each tone was played to both groups of chicks. The unfamiliar tone caused a visibly fearful reaction, but the familiar tone provoked no reaction.*

Evolution has taught to us animals, that we should be careful with unknown stimuli if we want to stay alive. This behaviour has been passed in some form or another to every member of a management team in the genes from those of our ancestors who managed to survive.

Court of identical members

Acceptance of differences is at the heart of all interaction. Humans are by nature afraid of the unknown, and fear separates and isolates. We humans have a strong need to see our own picture next to us, identical to what we see in ourselves. Therefore, it requires a strong presence, transparency and sensitivity, to be able to hear and see the richness of diversity.

Diversity is present in management all the time. One person wants exact instructions, another complete freedom. The variety of desires is endless. If the default mind-set is „they all are similar to me%ςthe need to see differences will not arise. The view displays only foggy similarities.

When similarity is taken to the extreme, it starts to control the operation of the team. Many management teams execute a kind of court ideology. A court is traditionally built on similarity. You have to share the same spirit or you do not fit in at the court at all. The royal court members must at least have a spiritual kinship to each other. The most important task is to serve the King at Court.

In modern times, the worshipping court group ingratiates and flatters the Director King, and their only goal is to stay in this society and enjoy the benefits of the old boy system. When one's position at court has been attained, no one dares to take the risk of challenging the king, as this may result in expulsion from court. After all, no one wants voluntarily to become an outsider.

Court makes war against divergence

Diversity is the core fuel for development of a team and the foundation of excellence for a Stellar Team. Paradoxically, however, we have a natural tendency to avoid differences. Therefore, this automatic reaction produces two basic options: (1) avoid diversity and strive always to move farther away, or (2) fight against diversity and prove the superiority of your own different way. We want to change others and mute differences. We are in a determined war against diversity.

> *A new member came to the management team in an expert organization, and with great enthusiasm and a hunger for reform he wanted to start developing his own responsibility area. In the management team his speeches were listened to tactfully for a few months, until the reality began to dawn.*
>
> *Some senior members of the management team communicated clearly to this innovator what they were thinking: „I̓ve been in this organization for more than 20 years, and the ideas you are suggesting are simply not fit for us. If they fit somewhere else, it doesnȆ mean that they would fit here. I just know it and I know this organization. It is better not to suggest those things here. Is that clear?„*
>
> *Another colleague went on the warpath against diversity: „Could we agree, that you care of your own business and you let me take care of mine. It is better for both of us‰*

Management teams are involved in a war against diversity. They have formed their own ways to fight against differences. The tendency to avoid differences manifests in various terms of how not to venture differing opinions. Here are some of the most typical patterns:

- Remain quiet and let things be, because, after all, nothing will change.
- Direct your attention to alternative action. When a colleague is presenting his case move your attention to your own thoughts or onto the secrets of the computer in front of you. An effective way of distancing yourself is to read mails while your colleague is speaking.
- Hum and create the impression that we agree. When the meeting is over you can start to wring your hands with another colleague over all the insanity of the meeting.

A more visible form of the war against diversity takes the form of an open battle against difference. Many management teams are passionate battlefields, where you hear attestations of individual superiority exploding and accusations against others whistling by.

The most civilized management teams fight cleanly with rational weapons and use a large part of their energy to keep emotions hidden beneath the surface. The battles are an actual series of concentrated fire: long commentaries and exhausting repetitions. The debate sounds like throwing automatic gainsaying grenades: It is – It isn't! The parties just dig deeper into their own trenches, and no ground is given voluntarily.

In less civilised management teams people dig into their boltholes equipped with harsh feelings and strong emotions. Disappointment at the contribution of a colleague appears either in the form of an exploding accusation or in a more cunning way with sneaky generalizations:

- Our sales department is always undervalued . . .
- I hear of dissatisfaction in the corridors all the time – and, in particular, from support functions. They feel that they are never appreciated.
- We should put more emphasis on management. People management is in certain parts of the organization below standard, really pathetic.

Heroes build peace

The Stellar Team does not wage war against diversity. A top team forms a peace-keeping force that uses adaptive methods of diplomacy against the hostilities. The best remedy against fear is to increase security and to remind people of our general status quo, where we no longer face primitive threats such as predators, frost and hostile enemy tribes. When differences are natural, security increases, and it is promoted by repeating the following facts:

- For the management team the utilization of diversity is the lifeblood and catalyst of development. If the difference is suppressed, it burns the energy of the team – in vain.
- Diversity always arouses emotions, and it is acceptable to express emotion levels in messages to colleagues. Each silenced emotion conceals an important issue or an action style, which could be a learning experience for the team as a whole.
- Diversity takes effort and it is worthwhile. A joy of cognitive flow produces, with similar people, common solutions that easily satisfy Hasty Intuition, but qualitatively significant solutions are generated when we bother to face up to the challenges presented by Deep Analysis in the company of different types of people.

The journey to a real Stellar Team demands that we overcome militancy towards diversity. We have to confront and utilize the dynamic forces of diversity. When people work longer together, differences will, without exception, arouse critical and unwelcome emotions. Tensions emerge between people. Depending on the team and the mutual relations of its members, tensions will be channelled into action that either destroys or constructs the team. – Even in peacekeeping forces, the management teams are not free of this phenomenon of group dynamics.

> WAKE UP! DIVERSITY IS NOT AN ADVANTAGE AUTOMATICALLY, IT IS A BURDEN! YOU WILL DERIVE THE BENEFIT OF DIVERSITY WHEN YOU ENTER INTO THE MINDSCAPE OF DIFFERENT PEOPLE

When curiosity wins over a member of management team and he or she decides to take the first step towards the worldview of someone different, an irreversible change takes place. It can begin, for example, with a question that just shows interest: What might be the background of that idea – would you tell me more? When curiosity appears in an appreciative way, there will be a reward waiting. The management team system begins to evolve when even one single member decides to change his or her way of operating. At its best, curiosity spreads and the understanding of the power of diversity will increase.

Look in the mirror

The diversity of the management team becomes visible if people agree to look in the mirror together. Individual operating styles can be categorized and they help discussion about individual differences within these styles. An analysis of operating style is not a personality test but it describes individual behaviour. Descriptions of operating styles must not be seen to value or criticize because no single operating style is better than another. Each style has its strengths and development areas.

Most of the operating style evaluations on the market are based on Jungian psychology, which has served as a background for the development of several concepts for business use. Sufficient simplification generates practical descriptions, which make clear the basic differences between individuals. Critically we can say that only dead people belong in boxes. In other words, all categorizing and classification is insulting to a living human being because he or she is not a type but rather a process.

Experience has shown, however, that the creation of stereotypes does serve the understanding of diversity. In order to increase this understanding we have chosen one of the frames of reference, the Peili™ behaviour profile which allows the management team to deal with the diversity of the team effectively. The quadrant of Peili™ consists of two axes:

A. The horizontal axis describes how much you use power in your interaction. You may be dominant or easy-going. Dominant takes space, the behaviour is assertive and straightforward. Easy-going gives space, the behaviour is observant and adapts to others.
B. The vertical axis describes how much you express emotions in your interaction. The behaviour is either formal or informal. Formal means systematic, fact oriented and neutral behaviour. Informal means, on the contrary, immediate emotional reactions, spontaneity and people centred behaviour.

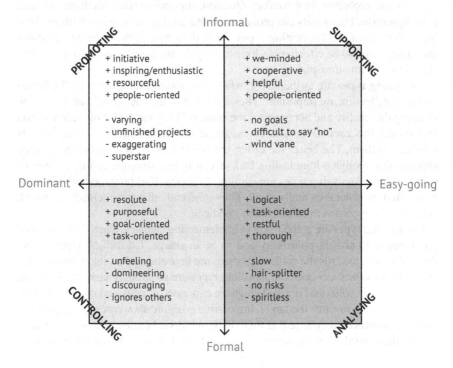

Promoting

+ initiative
+ inspiring/enthusiastic
+ resourceful
+ people-oriented

- varying
- unfinished projects
- exaggerating
- superstar

Supporting

+ we-minded
+ cooperative
+ helpful
+ people-oriented

- no goals
- difficult to say "no"
- wind vane

Dominant ← → Easy-going

Informal

Formal

Controlling

+ resolute
+ purposeful
+ goal-oriented
+ task-oriented

- unfeeling
- domineering
- discouraging
- ignores others

Analysing

+ logical
+ task-oriented
+ restful
+ thorough

- slow
- hair-splitter
- no risks
- spiritless

Figure 10.1 Different behavioural styles meet in management teams

Published with permission of Integro Oy.

Peili™ consists of four behavioural styles (see Figure 10.1): promoting, controlling, supporting and analysing styles.

Behavioural styles in practice

Promoting, controlling, supporting and analysing behaviours with different emphases can be found in every management team. Each style has its strengths and pitfalls, which can be detected very soon in the dynamics of a management team.

Promoting types are at their best when they are allowed to inspire and encourage others. In their team they are innovators, visionaries and daydreamers. The future is all the time full of opportunities. They make quick decisions and intuitive solutions, which are, if necessary, reversed the next day, as new ideas have now conquered the mind. Promoting types are often impatient. They are not at their best in organizing and creating systematics, because details are not their cup of tea. They also talk more than others do, and everything is possible in their thoughts. However, the realities of everyday life are easily forgotten.

Supporting types are at their best as interpreters of social situations and creators of team spirit. They are good network builders and loyal team players. Supporting types are happy to use tried solutions and tested practices in order to avoid troubles and problems. In a conflict situation, supporting types mediate and seek to compromise. They easily put problematic and hurting issues aside without dealing with them at all. Supporting types are at their best in maintaining the status quo. They can also be effective, as long as they do not have to sense pointless tensions in the team atmosphere.

Analysing types are at their best, when a thorough examination of the issues and deep reflection are important. They are often in the background and focus on ensuring the quality and accuracy of the matters. They have a lot of patience, and they do not fool around in vain. To assure, to ensure and again, to make sure is a natural to them. The better the order, the easier it is to breathe. Generally they appear calm, though a long lasting lack of clarity and structure can be a cause of pain for them. Analysing types are cautious in their self-expression and it is difficult to find out what they really think. They inherently distance themselves, which can easily be regarded as indifference to others.

Controlling types are at their best in implementing changes, when there is a need for someone to take responsibility and to be in charge. Controlling types propel things forward, towards the goals. Schedules are kept and useless interpersonal dramas will not slow them down. Controlling types are so strongly task-oriented, that others get easily bulldozed down. Things are expressed directly and openly, in order to move forward, towards the target. Impossible goals are showcases that add fuel to their fire. However, they note that they do things alone because others cannot keep up with their speed. They are loners, who sometimes lose their situational awareness.

Management team is a sum of styles

Diversity always enables „the risk of unintentional insult‰If the management team members approach the others only from their own behavioural style, they do not benefit from diversity. This only leads to the formation of defence positions and competition to see who will have the last word. On the other hand, if there are many members with the same style, collaboration works without greater friction but the benefits of different styles do not become visible. As food for thought we will describe four fictional teams, in which all the members represent the same style.

A promoting management team is innovative, energetic and creative. There is however a lack of competences in anticipation, patience and in the completion of tasks. A particular challenge for this team lies in creating common goals and house rules, and sticking to them. A promoting team will spiral out of control as soon as it gets a chance.

A controlling management team is efficient, productive and goal-oriented. On the other hand, it has a lack of competence in collaboration, human relationships and creating visions. A particular challenge is to make the team play towards a common goal. In this team everyone wants to be the leader and the pace is hot!

An analysing management team is precise, thoughtful and analytical. It lacks competence in interaction, courage and decision-making. Its particular challenge is to move the team into productive action. Slow operations and an overflow of details may prevent this team from achieving success – they do not see the big picture behind the details.

The supporting management team builds a great spirit and focuses on amenities and the function of interpersonal relationships. There is a lack of competence in goal-orientation, decision-making and efficiency. This team̂s particular challenge is in the transition into courageous and goal-oriented action. Taking responsibility and dealing with negative issues is the hardest thing for this team.

VISIBLE DIFFERENCES: Try these, if you dare

1. Take the Peili table (Figure 10.1) as starting point for a discussion on how each of you sees himself/herself. Position yourselves in the quadrant.
2. Focus on each member of your management team separately. Give feedback to each other and try to find the „right‰place for everyone (of course it can be the same as in the self-evaluation).
3. Explore the distribution in behavioural styles: What are your conclusions? How does that distribution appear in your daily work? What are your strengths? And pitfalls?
4. Use the diversity: Discuss how you can counteract the pitfalls from preventing your collaboration? If one quadrant of the table is empty, which one of you has those strengths most inherently? If the team is too much in the same box, how do you take care of the people in other quadrants?

Management teams typically represent dominating behaviour. Controlling and promoting behavioural styles form the majority in management teams and they create the basis for thinking and operating, connected to their behavioural style. If there are no supporting and analysing members, a significant part of opportunities to be gained from diversity will remain concealed. A real Stellar Team is created only when a team consciously wants to put an effort into taking advantage of diversity. Diversity must be seen as abundance, not as a burden.

Mary, CEO in an expert organization, had been in charge of the business for years. The line-up of the management team had been changed year after year but one thing had remained almost unchanged: the majority of the members were men. For the last few years, she had been leading a team of seven men. She had consciously chosen different individuals for her team, and that gave new dynamics to operations. Next, she decided to take gender distribution onto her agenda. She did not want to be the only female in the team because she recognized that the team had impossible expectations of her. She was supposed to be warm, motherly and accessible, and at the same time a strong flag bearer and assertive decision-maker. Finally, Mary stated in her coaching session that she was leading „seven dwarfs‰and she was ready for the change.

Influencing the structure of the management team

The structure and members of the management team change often. Typically, when the CEO changes, the structure is renewed at the same time. People in charge also tot up attractive offers from head-hunters and transit from one management team to another. Sometimes underachievement is also a good reason for a quick change. The same goes for the shaky position of CEO.

The management team traditionally forms a group of „assistants for the CEO‰ New thinking in coaching leadership has increased the empowerment and the significance of the team, and the Stellar Team takes joint responsibility for this success. This is shared leadership. This may also shake up our traditional ways of thinking: Why should a team leader alone be responsible for choosing team members? What if the whole team were to participate in the recruitment of a new member? Joint discussion could start with following questions:

- Which operating style and way of thinking are we missing the most now?
- Which operating style do we need more of, to be able to ensure achievement of our present goals?
- Who would be credible candidates within our organization?

A Stellar Team makes more choices together! If the CEO decides on all employment alone, there is a big risk of choosing employees that match his/her own behavioural style. The management team should frankly fear similarity as regards the make-up of the team. Otherwise 1+1 will never be more than 2.

In the management team of a listed company there was a need for change. The team was far too big and they were missing the spark in their operation. CEO John was thinking about the options of how to shrink the team. In his conversation with his coach he came to a conclusion, to involve the whole management team. After the team had first defined their goal and the reason for their existence, they went on to the ideal number of members. Their thoughts on an efficient team were very much alike: they should have 2–3 members fewer than now.

The discussion went on, focusing on competences demanded by the common goals. The discussion was not only about substantial competences, but also about operating styles. It was important to ensure that different styles would be broadly represented. Finally, the members of the team wrote down on ballots the names of those they thought would be best suitable in the present situation and who they suggested stay in the team. The team made the decision, which was finally confirmed by John.

Conflicts are "business as usual"

> A conflict is a situation where people have uncompromising interests, goals or
> emotions
>
> (Ristikangas and Junkkari 2011: 60)

Diversity in management teams sparks and develops tensions and disagreement
for sure. Troublesome guys terrorize meetings and, between certain individuals,
a fire breaks out in no time. Different ways of thinking and operating continuously generate challenges for team collaboration. Diversity does not explain all
the tensions in teams, there are plenty of other reasons. So the question is: Why
do management teams get stuck and need to slow down? Where does the internal
friction in the team come from?

Unclear goals blur the vision

The collective performance of the team is based on how well its members collaborate for a common purpose. If the goal is ambiguous and obscure, the team
is confused and attention moves on to trivial issues. In addition, it is important to
remember that the goal rarely remains unchanged, as understanding increases, for
example, of market situation and other variables connected to the goal. Priorities
may change, and, at the same time also, goals may reveal new dimensions. If there
are no regular updating discussions, individual interpretations will start to assert
themselves and total blockage is only a matter of time. Frustration and tensions
start to spring up. The less there are clarifying conversations about goals, the more
there will be wrangles about those same goals.

Attitude handicap is crippling

A management team needs to take collective responsibility to dig out the potential of the team. If individual performers bury joint responsibility, conflict is
then only a matter of time. Which one of the following descriptions resembles
you most?

> A: As a member of the management team I am a part of an important team
> at company level, and the success of that team requires my full input – my
> competence and my leadership. In addition we need every member of this
> team to achieve our demanding goals.
> B: My role is important. I have the right competences and I know what
> I must do. I surely take care of my responsibilities and this does not depend
> on others or their actions. I know that the CEO or the leader of our manage-
> ment team takes care that other members of the team will give their best to
> the game.

If you recognize more the qualities of A, you are a member of a potential Stellar
Team. If, however, you recognize more the characteristics of B, you are potentially

an independent star. The synergy of collaboration is not being used. So, are you more of a star by yourself, or do you want to make stars of the others?

Mark was a long time management team member and he was in charge of the most significant business area of the company. He was an experienced old hand who had a wide customer network. Mark̂s attention was on customers and ensuring their satisfaction.

In the organization Mark̂s way of working aroused a lot of resentment. His style was very controlling and he did not give much of a say to others. Around the water cooler the comments were that he was a king, whose ideas were not to be challenged or questioned. If somebody dared to do so, this would result in systematic suppression as well as cunning slings and arrows.

Howard, the new leader of the management team recognized very quickly Mark̂s way of operating and its influence on management teamwork. Mark was a ÂhinoÊin the team and others were afraid of him. They shut their mouths and prepared to shelter themselves from Mark̂s revenge. As these dynamics became apparent in the management team development process, Howard was ready to take the necessary action to correct the situation. In a structural change Mark̂s position was lowered and his role was changed. Howard was prepared to take on Mark̂s counteroffensive and he was capable of keeping Mark under his control. After six months of fighting the situation had calmed down and Mark had adapted to his new role.

Incompetence frustrates

In a management team, an absolute advantage will be gained by the widespread combination of individual competences. The competences required must be based on goals and it is crystal clear that sole determination and hard work do not always lead to goals. There is a strong need for a wide spectrum of different competences in the team.

If the necessary competences are not available in the team, they must be acquired for each project separately. If the identified shortages in competences are not dealt with, there will be sparks and lightning among the members of the team. Missing competences lead to underachievement, which fuels very effectively internal tensions in the team.

Changes confuse the team

Management positions are shaky and the dream of having a „permanent%team is just wishful thinking. Head hunters poach leaders, there are natural transitions, the team is changed for one reason or another. An unchanged management team is realistically ancient history dating from the last millennium.

As changes happen, the team is exposed to new conflicts. Each member who joins or leaves the team has a remarkable effect on team dynamics. A new member always makes the entire team into a new team. Existing members need to create a relationship with the newcomer, and the new member respectively starts to create collaboration with several people. At the same time the newcomer will also influence the balance of power in the team. Filling old boots takes some amount of energy, depending on who has left the team.

A new member is also a new opportunity. He or she will sense very quickly the working culture and how to act in the team. If he or she is not filled in on goals and operating styles, integration will not happen. If the newcomer is active, not necessarily deliberately, in presenting new thoughts and development ideas, a counterforce will emerge after the honeymoon period.

An IT company had hired Thomas as vice president to be responsible for growth in a new business area. Thomas had worked in similar roles earlier and he was known as innovative and decisive in taking responsibilities. For the first couple of months the management team was nodding and was cautiously happy with the new hire. When ideas were supposed to be brought into practice, a clear separation in old and new members was revealed within the team. The enthusiasm of the newcomer was tested and he was clearly challenged. Finally the situation became unbearable and this talented expert left the company. Thomas could not stand the endless „grinding‰ with the old geezers.

Time pressure plays on the nerves

The most common threat against the formation of a Stellar Team is lack of time. He who is hasty will make mistakes – that‚s just the way it is. Agendas are run through according to tight schedules and they can leave bruises that may get infected. Offenses are often totally unintentional. After a period of festering the old insults will burst out in some later connection.

Lack of leadership creates shaky ground

An essential competence of leadership is the ability to act upon identified problems. If there is no culture of discipline and intervention, the management team ends up creating a tense atmosphere. Of course the leader of the team is primarily responsible for seizing upon problems and unwanted behaviour. On the other hand, if this responsibility is pushed solely to the highest director, there will not be a trace of a Stellar Team. When the members of the management team themselves intervene against the breaking of common rules, they create a counter force against indiscipline. The star begins to shine.

WAKE UP! GROWN UPS REALLY CAN PLAY IN THE SAME PLAYGROUND AND SEE TO IT THAT NO ONE HITS A FRIEND IN THE HEAD WITH A SAND SHOVEL.

Overcoming the fear of conflicts

All of the previously described six factors sensitize the management team to conflicts. At some point, tensions become tangible and visible in the team atmosphere. No relief will be forthcoming by dealing with the situation according to a basic human characteristic: we want to avoid conflicts. In tricky situations we do all we can to keep up a positive atmosphere and enjoyable life.

Regrettably that is not the way to solve the problem and tensions do not disappear that way. At best, we can sneak them down to deeper levels, hidden away from our active consciousness. There they will wait for the moment when the shield breaks or for when an innocent passer-by comes along with an excavator.

Fear of conflicts is one of the worst enemies of a Stellar Team (Lencioni 2002). The differences are clear between an ordinary management team and a Stellar Team that has overcome the fear of conflicts (Table 10.1).

There is only one way to overcome the fear of conflicts. You have to learn to face the fear and you have to begin to practice dealing with conflicts. In many organizations conflicts are taboos and they are avoided to the bitter end. The higher you go in hierarchies, the more you will see management teams who use enormous energy to conceal their conflicts.

WAKE UP! IS THERE ANY SENSE AT ALL? THE LONGER YOU HIDE A CONFLICT, THE MORE SURE YOU CAN BE THAT IT WILL BURST OUT INTO A BLOODY FIGHT BETWEEN PEOPLE.

Table 10.1 Fear of conflicts in practice.

Management team avoiding conflicts	*Stellar Team facing conflicts*
Passive and boring meetings	Open discussion where emotions are not hidden
Talking behind the back	Straightforward and appreciative communication
Avoiding sensitive issues	Dealing actively with problems
Keeping quiet although there would be something to say	Taking up critical and even sensitive issues
Affectation, untruthfulness, pleasing others	Honesty, minimized „politicking‰

Organizations used to believe that contradictions and conflicts automatically weakened productivity in a team. Conflicts were supposed to prevent the team from focusing on its tasks – and indeed, this was the case. If a conflict had developed onto a personal level, action in the management team was paralyzed. If, on the contrary, conflict remains sufficiently at a factual level, it will produce efficiency (De Dreu et al. 2003) and higher quality of decisions at management team level (Olson 2007). Conflicts between people in turn weaken trust and productivity in the team (Rispens et al. 2007). If disagreements between individuals are not tackled, they begin to influence the activities of the team, whether you try to hide them or not. The effects are palpable.

When fear of conflicts subsides and conflicts are treated as a natural part of cooperation, you will be progressing again on your way to the stars. You will get good results, if you accept conflicts as a part of daily interaction. Things are handled objectively because action and results create more motivation than individual differences in operating styles.

Conflict competence is a team skill

Fear of conflicts keeps most mouths shut. However, all of us do not regard conflict as being equally dreadful. We are different, and additionally, sensitivity to dealing with conflicts is affected by the quality of the relationships. The more there is trust, the more safely you can deal with difficult issues. It is easier to handle contradictions with people who are more familiar. Spouses are a good example of this. The better you can solve your conflicts, the stronger the ground for your relationship will be. The ability to handle conflicts is a key skill in all relationships.

Taken to a management team level, the ability to deal with conflicts moves into new dimensions. Firstly, controlling a conflict in a team is much more difficult. Group dynamics are always unique and every single member in the team influences them through his or her way of thinking and acting. Also the commitment to the team and the guiding power of a common goal add their characteristic tone to team action.

Individual abilities of team members to deal with conflicts do not correlate to the team's skill level in this regard. The conflict competence of a team is built on the same basis as in a bilateral relationship. The more there is trust, the better issues will be handled and named by their real names.

Conflict competence grows with practice, so it can be developed. A team develops its conflict competence when it is exposed to handling the most difficult situations. A Stellar Team does not fear conflicts but they are taken as opportunities to learn and to create something new – as a team. The more there is courage and risk-taking capacity in the team, the more certain development will be.

A Stellar Team has overcome the most typical factors that prevent conflict competence at a team level: fear and pseudo efficiency. The most typical fear is that talking about an issue will hurt a colleague. Avoidance may also be caused by the fear of becoming isolated or set aside, if you start to take up issues in a too direct manner. Fear may even be caused by the uncertainty of how a colleague will react. You cannot be too sure of your own reactions either. Thus, plenty of fears.

The medicine for fear is security. If fear takes over, security structures have not proved strong enough. A Stellar Team has overcome conflict fears through systematic work on developing security, which builds mutual trust. When there is enough confidence between the members of the team, the effect of practicing conflict competence will be visible in results, too.

The Stellar Team has an advantage over the other potential hindrance, the pseudo efficiency, which goes alongside with the fears. Many management team members declare to themselves their desire to be effective and they consider this as a good motive to avoid conflicts. In the background is the belief that conflicts consume the efficiency of the team. However, the same conflict avoiders are often willing to go on and on about missing functionality of the team with their favourite colleague and to use their energy in complaining. If annoyances cannot be dealt with at work, the bad feeling will be channelled in the end outside the workplace and into the home.

> **Remember!** RESEARCH SHOWS THAT CONFLICTS, WHICH YOU HAVE FACED AND HANDLED CONSTRUCTIVELY, WILL INCREASE THE OUTPUT OF THE ENGINE OF YOUR STELLAR TEAM!

Ideas for overcoming fear of conflicts

How can a management team develop its ability to handle conflicts constructively? The most important thing is to recognize the opportunity that a conflict may be productive. In addition, it is good to admit that there are numerous factors at individual and team level, which have the ability to prevent you from facing conflicting sensitive situations.

After clarifying your mind-set, the actual practice of conflict competence is much easier. It is good to discuss the rules for testing thoroughly. So the question is: What do we have to agree upon, in order to be able to handle even sensitive issues in our meetings? Typically the agreed items are connected to the following themes.

- Confidentiality – Subject matters remain as information for our management team only.
- The right to a time out – Everyone has the right to ask for a break or a time-out, in order to avoid the overheating of a situation.
- Enabling encounters – Recapping on a dissenting opinion provides assurance that the opinion has been heard. Everyone has a duty to empower others and to ensure that they are correctly understood.
- Processing own emotions – Everyone has an obligation to speak on their own behalf and through their own feelings.
- Appreciative approach – Everyone appreciates others and primarily seeks to understand, not to blame or judge.

• The Messenger – Everyone has an obligation to take controversial issues for debate, as soon they are identified. Being a messenger is a precious gift to the team.

When the rules are clear, even the most sensitive conflict themes can be taken safely for processing. If plain rules and playing according to them is not enough, you can use different variations and mutual agreements, which will ensure that the conflicts stay on a secure ground. Next, we will present some ideas in the form of prearranged roles, which can be used in the daily work of your management team.

Minesweeper

The team selects a person who is given special authorization to lift up the hidden mines. This person has courage enough to broach the most sensitive issues in order to initiate a discussion of them in accordance with the agreed rules.

Referee

One of the team members takes the role of referee, who takes care that the action is according to the rules. The referee has a special right to interrupt the situation at any time, in order to ensure that the game will go on by the rules. It is good to notice that the referee does not have to be the supervisor of the team, anybody of the team can take this important responsibility.

Meaning amplifier

The minesweeper will also need the other members to take responsibility in order to keep the handling of a conflict in the right proportions. The role of the meaning amplifier is needed when the situation begins to move clearly into an area of discomfort. Then the meaning amplifier will discontinue the situation and point out that the processing of the current conflict is very meaningful for the team. This role may sound a little strange, but in an emotional debate it is good to take some distance, and to find a rational perspective for the conflict process.

The processing of a conflict succeeds best when as many as possible of the team members take the responsibility of strengthening the action by the rules. The more there are active quality inspectors, the better you will reach the common goal.

In order to broaden understanding of conflict competence, we recommend that your management team does some operating style analysis connected to diversity. Many of them seem to be based on Jungian philosophy. As examples we can mention MBTI® with different applications, and DiSC®, Insights®, Peili™ and several analysis models that specialize in operating styles. All of them include the idea of how to approach different individuals in a tense situation.

Development is possible

Conflict competence will develop, if it is allowed opportunities. The better the team leader knows him/herself, the more likely the team will learn to deal with future conflicts. If the team leader gets stuck in a conflict situation, the team will not have much possibility to influence the situation. If an inability to deal with the situation is seen only in other members of the management team, the problem is not severe, as the leader is responsible for the process and he/she will promote the issue systematically – at least in a Stellar Team.

Summary of conflict competence in the Stellar Team:

- Tensions and conflicts will emerge always when a group of people come together – sooner or later.
- A Stellar Team is capable of dealing with conflicts. There are different approaches to team conflicts in theories of team development. Dealing with conflicts is a team skill.
- Conflict competence describes the know-how, which grows in the team through common practice. What is essential is how the team wants to learn to deal with conflicts. If there is no motivation, issues will be swept under the carpet, and the team will imagine that everything is all right.
- A Stellar Team knows how to handle conflicts at an early stage, before they escalate to personal conflicts, and in this way it is able to keep them at a factual level.

TRY THIS: Bring up for discussion

Select one of your colleagues. Name one issue or phenomenon that you donß want to talk about with your colleague, even though you know he/she is aware of it. What would change if that thing you named did not exist? How would that thing change if you brought it up for discussion? How could you do that? When?

---

11 Feedback puts wings on development

SILO INFLAMMATION

Symptoms: Isolation, avoidance of collaboration, solo playing

Silo inflammation is a well-known disease in many management teams. *Silo inflammation* is best recognized by the fact that between meetings the members of the management team potter around in their own silos and focus on issues concerning their own teams. The inflammation causes vanishing interest in dealing with colleagues. Also, common issues in the management team look distant. *Silo inflammation* spreads very easily and if left untreated, it will infect the entire organization by causing people to isolate themselves in their silos, avoiding distracting initiatives to cooperate with other departments or business units. In the management team *silo inflammation* manifests itself in the duration of focus on action for the common good, which scarcely lasts the time of a standard meeting. Infected patients can put up with the others in the same room for only a few hours a month. In between the meetings the inflammation will surely keep the members apart.

Care instructions in Appendix 2: ÂSelf care guide for management teamsÊ

People talk a lot about feedback and its importance, and there is hardly any leadership training without that theme. It is easy to talk about feedback; however transforming this form of wisdom into daily activity is another story. The progress of a Stellar Team will degenerate if feedback is not included in common interaction. Without feedback we will stand alone with our own interpretations, and we either sink into self-satisfaction or adapt ourselves to the status quo, deeper than ever. Galactic dimensions of enthusiasm and development will remain untapped without feedback.

Feedback is an important part of the communication system in the management team. Internal feedback culture is built with every encounter. The core of the management team feedback practices is how to give, ask for and receive feedback.

Systems offer opportunities for operations

A system is constructed by details that are connected to each other, and their relations are controlled in interaction. Theories of interaction emphasize that people do not react to action itself but to the meaning brought about by the action. Interaction can be split into fragments and separate elements, but practically, these elements seem to build a system, which produces meaning.

> *My colleague Andy (1) said „good morning‰(2) his tone was friendly and (3) he looked at his mobile at the same time. This system brought about by his actions, gave me, as observer, the meaning „not very appreciative‰ even though the single actions in that system were mostly positive.*

The above-mentioned observation creates a less inspiring mark in the internal system of an individual. A team forms a system, consisting of the internal systems of each individual. If the system of a team has a large lack of appreciation, it is of no use to expect enthusiasm in the meeting. Initiating enthusiasm in the team demands individuals who start thinking with systems intelligence (Saarinen and Hämäläinen 2004). The more there are people who take responsibility to influence the system, the more the system will evolve and develop. First we need someone to step up, then others will come, and finally there will be many.

Systems intelligent way of initiating change in a system called a team

1. **Believe that the team is able to achieve more and much better than now**
   It is good to look at what a team produces, and also, to look at what it does not produce. The team may produce something with full steam, for example, a „strategy‰At the same time, all that is not „strategy‰is not produced. In this way, the action leads to a result, where nothing other than „strategy‰ is being born, e.g. a decision to change PR office, a discussion about an ice hockey game, customer feedback analysis, evaluation of competence charts, etc.

   The concepts of „being born‰and „not being born‰make it possible for us to notice that each choice we make also restricts a lot of other choices. By choosing a certain road we choose not to choose other roads. Following this choice, every new act requires a new choice. So we can choose again and again, what will come into being and what will not. Choices generate a self-supporting mechanism, which protects itself against choices from outside the choices („strategy‰vs. „not-strategy‰

Harry believed that his colleagues in the management team had latent potential and he started to imagine what the team could achieve at its best. He noticed that what was „not being born%«n the team was enthusiastic, flow-like co-creation. Then he was immediately able to identify the force that prevented „not being born%«o be born. The team's own actions made this impossible again and again, by setting over-long agendas and unrealistic schedules for their meetings.

2. **Feel dissatisfaction with the uninspired atmosphere or the weak productivity of the team**

   The starting point for dissatisfaction is the experience that the present system of the team does not support achieving something better. In that situation, you may note that the members of the team can choose whether they want to inspire or discourage the team. A negative choice is often made unintentionally, through carelessness and thoughtlessness.

Harry saw the uninspired situation in the management team as temporary, because the possibilities of the situation were controlled by systems that could be affected.

3. **Be aware of the basics of the system that controls the situation**

   Everything that people do in a visible system of interaction is transformed through the experience of each person involved, into a component of an internal, invisible system of each individual involved. In their internal systems people carry, in addition to present observations, a great number of historical observations, interpretations and meanings. The interaction will be the sum of visible and internal, invisible systems.

   In these internal systems you can find common features and characteristics that can be generalized, although their meanings and interpretations may deviate remarkably. Individually valuable meanings are mostly universal and common to all human beings. That is why enthusiasm is caused rather by variables of a situation than by personal special characteristics.

Harry focused on interaction. He knew that everybody needed appreciation, acceptance, security, social connectedness and community. Harry noted that emotional intelligence, systems thinking and sensitivity to the situation offered a means to influence the invisible factors through visible systems. Harry saw the management team as a human system, in which he also was a component.

4.   Take courageous measures to modify the system
Destabilizing or changing a system is actually easy. It usually requires deviant behaviour, for instance in everyday situations. Systems intelligent action
often seems trivial but its effects are revolutionary. The system starts to
change, when a part of it is changed.

Harry planned a series of small but concrete acts for the meetings of his
management team:

1.   *I will act enthusiastically in our next regular meeting – I will act differ-*
     ently also in the future, behaving in a way „wrongly‰
2.   *I will suggest that we no longer strive to sell larger deliveries but*
     smaller – I will also begin to present „irrational‰options every now
     and then.
3.   *I'm going to start calling our customers „members of our orchestra‰-*
     I will begin to give totally new names for known concepts.

5.   Let the systemic change force influence the whole team
As you influence the conscious enthusiasm in the team, they start to understand that this team or this situation could be something more. The phases
described earlier will then start, i.e. (1) the insight of „not being born‰oppor-
tunities, (2) dissatisfaction with the uninspiring situation, (3) the understanding of the system that controls the situation and (4) taking small actions.
Social norms do not allow deviant behaviour, so your small action can be just
a slight elevation of your own enthusiasm.

It is better to start with a small step. Saarinen often talks about elevating
phenomena and uses clear examples of those: a little longer eye contact when
greeting the other, slightly more rigorous listening to the other, or just one appreciative word. A small change in your own enthusiasm will multiply and spread,
and then generate a big increase in the team̂s enthusiasm level. According to
the mathematical idea of J.T. Bergqvist the level will raise from 0.8 to 1.2. (See
Chapter 2.)
The team may become inspired unconsciously, while it just carries on with the
situation. In the internal experiences of the team members, the system will be
redefined in a new way, for example, „our management team is, after all, an open,
creative and inspiring team‰Thus the invisible system has been altered, which
will change personal interpretation and experience.
As there are more and more inspiring situations, the management team becomes
more enthusiastic and more productive. Systems dictatorship and organizational
culture can be developed into a system of Superproductivity, when becoming
inspired is designed to be a systematic occurrence.

CHANGE THE SYSTEM: Could you be the first "Someone"?

Read this out loud for yourself:
Our management team could be more and better. Thatîs why we are dissatisfied. The interaction in our management team could be better. We need small actions, which will be initiated by Someone. I am that Someone.
– Could Someone read this out loud to his/her colleagues?

Correct your understanding

Powered by systems thinking the Stellar Team moves on to the frequency of feedback. As every member of the management team is capable of writing with laudable grades an essay on the essence and practices of feedback, we approach this theme from a different perspective. We explore what kind of changes we should accomplish in our thinking, in order to influence our ways of giving and receiving feedback. These provocative ideas apply to every management team, no matter if the team is fresh or experienced. Which of the following thought patterns do you recognize as individuals or as a management team?

"Feedback is a task of a supervisor" – *Correct and incorrect!*

A supervisor gives feedback and a subordinate receives it. In a management team the leader is supposed to give feedback to the members of the team. Thatîs it. It seems totally impossible that in a management team somebody would give feedback to a colleague. The colleague might even feel offended. This is the normal way of thinking in almost every organization.

The management team that wants to develop itself as a team sees the world differently. Giving feedback belongs obviously to everybody. Let us look at this from the perspective of an interaction system. In Figure 11.1 you can see two models of a management team. In the picture on the left, the arrows come from the leader of the team, who is typically the supervisor of all management team members. This is the person whose task it is to give feedback. In bilateral discussions, most typically in performance reviews, the feedback channel is open and feedback skills are exercised – at best in both directions.

Privately given feedback is very seldom transmitted to the team. The CEO has created more or less confidential relationships with his subordinates, and feedback and discussions are better with some, less good with others.

The bilateral relationships, which are important for building a team, are nearly invisible. The closest trustees of the CEO admittedly receive more attention in meetings than others, and the poor objects of trust deficit are left to oblivion or they just get some critical whiplashes. The world of the management team looks very much one-dimensional.

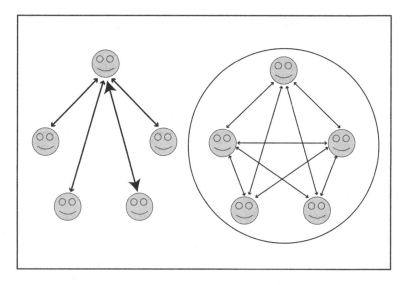

Figure 11.1 Feedback system of a management team (a) and (b)

In the right hand side picture everyone is responsible for giving feedback. Instead of four feedback arrows there are now 10 feedback relationships, which is 2.5 times more. This enables mutual development of feedback. Feedback is seen as an important part of the action and development of the team.

> **Hey there**, imagine this: that each member of your team were a mirror which reflected you and your own actions, whether successful or not. As there would be many mirrors around you, you would get reflections from different perspectives and in different ways. The personal mirrors are different. In an inveterate management team the mirrors would not show anything useful, because they would be so darkened and even distorted. In a Stellar Team everyonês duty is to keep the mirror clear and available, as well as to make use of otherŝreflections.

We are as human beings, quite pleased by the idea of being surrounded by grown up people who would genuinely be interested in us and our doings. If the feedback culture of the team is not very advanced, pleasure will be replaced by fear. I wonder what they think of me? Where are they going to direct their attention now?

To develop a functioning feedback culture, everyone in the team is primarily obliged to share lots of positive feedback in the team. In addition, everyone is also obliged to give wise feedback on their observations of issues that need improvement. The development of the team will take a leap forward as soon as feedback is not seen only as a duty of the supervisor, but of everyone.

"Critical feedback must be given privately and positive feedback openly in the team" – *Incorrect!*

This catchword has been repeated in feedback trainings for years. There are certainly situations in which this instruction is suitable, but what will follow if this idea guides a management team? The team starts hushing and whitewashing things. They learn to nod as a sign of unity in spite of disagreement. The team becomes underachieving, because corrective feedback has been transferred from within common discussions to quiet debates at water coolers and in hallways.

The management team which is on its way to the stars exercises all manner of feedback. Examples of top performance are teams who are capable of giving even negative feedback in the team. There should be no space for hushing in any organization, certainly at least not at management team level. Successes must be handled but poor quality/weak performance/bad behaviour must also be seized upon – at the team level.

The effects are tangible when the management team dares to take steps, particularly when giving critical team feedback. When feedback is appreciative, there will be no need to hide behind feedback mirrors. We must face the feedback messages and deal with them. Every feedback is an opportunity, a gift from a colleague. Why shouldn't I pause and explore the beneficial learning that it could provide to me?

Feedback in the team must not be solely negative. Findings in positive psychology research are very useful when giving negative feedback. We will achieve the best results when the amount of positive feedback is approximately triple that of critical. Marcial Losada and other researchers warn us: if there is only positive feedback and no critical feedback, the effect of feedback and productivity of the team will sink dramatically (Losada and Heaphy 2004; Fredrickson and Losada 2005). Even top performers may become underachievers.

"Results of leadership feedback surveys are private" – *Incorrect!*

Organizations continuously perform all kinds of leadership evaluations. 360-degree feedback is a standard in management teams. As everybody gets feedback from their own subordinates, they must analyse the feedback together with their own teams. If the supervisor of a supervisor is interested in results, it is possible to revert to the report in the personal performance review. Every member of the management team has the responsibility to go through the results with their own troops and to make the necessary conclusions.

Unfortunately, experience has shown that managers and executives can be divided roughly into three groups according to their compliance with the guidelines described above:

- 1/3 of supervisors are so well informed that they discuss with subordinates and act more or less as they should.

– 1/3 of supervisors are respectively those who, because of their own insecurity, incompetence or reluctance, do nothing at all with the feedback they receive. The report goes on their shelves to gather dust.

– 1/3 of supervisors are somewhere in between the previous two. If they have a conversation on the basis of the feedback, it is very superficial. Typically, they can say they have carried out the task, but without any giving added value to anyone.

Why on earth does the feedback go into hiding on the shelves, and why does anybody justify to themselves that it is a personal thing? We can find varying reasons for this phenomenon, one of which is linked more widely to the feedback culture of the organization. What is the actual atmosphere like for handling feedback within organizations?

It is a general principle in feedback processes that the responses must remain anonymous. Feedback givers are protected, and this is to ensure that feedback is as honest as possible. It usually requires at least five persons to answer, in order to make it impossible to identify individual answers in the average curves. However, despite this good intention, the everyday reality often appears to be quite different. Here are a few examples.

1. In the 180-degree feedback process of a management team in a communications company it was noted, that the feedback culture was not very advanced and the management team wanted to work on it together. They decided to ask a selected group of employees for feedback on their coaching leadership approach. They used Coaching Leadership Pulse as a survey, an evaluation produced by BoMentis Oy.

The end of the survey period was at hand and a member of the management team had received only a few responses, although a lot of reminders had been sent out to his staff. In spite of these reminders the response rate remained quite low. Finally there came an explanation when one of the employees who had been reminded called the survey organizer:

„I am not going to give feedback to my supervisor. If I said what I think, I would suffer from that immediately. I talked to those who had already given their responses and they had come to a decision to give only positive feedback. Our common idea is, the sooner we get over this and the less this gets attention, the better for us. None of us wants to become the object of unwelcome attention from our supervisor.‰

The feedback culture of this organization was very immature. Unfortunately the same applies to many other organizations, too.

2. The management team of a company in the construction business was asking for feedback from middle management. One of those supervisors crystallized the feedback culture very impressively:

„Leadership feedback is sheer screwing around. Nobody gives real feedback in those 360s. If I did it and my supervisor knew that Iˆm disappointed with his operations, that would affect my career and my incentives immediately. I would be finished for sure and would need a new job. So why should I be so stupid and tell you what I really think?‰

Within these immature feedback cultures lies a common belief that feedback is personal. The results are unbearable. Even today, huge amounts of money get wasted in getting fake responses from anonymous responders. Also the people receiving feedback do their duties routinely and merely report the summary of feedback in a couple of minutes in their team meeting. Unfortunately that is all.

In a Stellar Team giving feedback is expressly a method of common learning. When there is enough trust, the management team is able to give feedback without the protection of anonymity. All the feedback must be processed together with your employees – always. You can never be in such a hurry or prioritize something else, so that there is no time for processing the feedback. If the supervisor does not use time for developing his/her own leadership practices, that gives a clear signal: development is not important, and by the way, your feedback was worth nothing!

TEST THIS: Processing your own feedback

When you come to your own evaluation of your leadership style, proceed by taking these steps:

I   Prepare yourself

  –   Go through your feedback and pick up the points that make you thoughtful. Either you are not totally sure where this feedback comes from, or you just want to hear more of these competence areas. Select 2–5 items.
  –   Pick up the points, with which you are particularly satisfied. It is good to find several of these, e.g. 3. Write them down separately.
  –   Discuss your feedback with a colleague. Show him/her your report and create a culture of openness. Reflect with your colleague on your thoughts for the upcoming processing by analysing dialogue with your team. The aim is to prepare your mind for that important meeting.

–   Reserve time for a dialogue with your people and tell them that the subject is your leadership feedback. You can also send them the summary of the feedback in advance. If you decide to send the report electronically, it is better to remove the open comments in the feedback. The most important thing is that it gives your employees the opportunity to orientate themselves for the upcoming discussion.

II   Face-to-face dialogue of the feedback with your team

–   The dialogue has two goals: (1) You create a model to develop an open feedback culture and (2) you achieve, through the eyes of the others, a deeper understanding of your leadership.

–   The dialogue can be accelerated towards those goals with the following ideas:

o   Express frankly your gratitude for the feedback, thank these people for the effort they have taken for your sake.

o   The more people talk, the better. Your duty is to enable the discussion.

o   Ask your people to talk freely and express in their own words where they think you are at your best. Positivity builds connections and it will make it easier to say even negative things directly later on.

o   Ask people first to chat in pairs or groups of 3, in order to get everybody involved. It is then easier to share an opinion of a pair or a group than a separate feedback of one's own.

o   Look for everyday experiences of the employees, where your selected characteristic or competence area is in use or respectively not in use. The more concrete way you get inside those situations, the better you will enter into the thoughts and experiences of your people.

o   This is not a place for your explanations or defending yourself. Ask questions and listen to answers. Analyse together particularly those points you selected in advance for further investigation. Asking questions is good for that.

o   Talking about development goals is also important. Let people talk, thank them for all that they are saying. The more they dare to raise up critical voices, the more they will trust you. (Congratulate yourself on the trust you have earned!)

o   Thank them for their confidence and promise them to come back to the discussion with your conclusions in the near future.

- The discussion has probably given you so much to digest that you may want to use a couple of days to consider all those things.

III After the feedback dialogue

Crystallize the core of the feedback in a few points.

o Where are you at your strongest? How could you use that strength even more widely?

o In which development area do you want to put your energy? What kind of action plan are you going to make for that? What will your behaviour look like when you have achieved that state? Where do you need to put in extra effort to achieve the goal?

Try this! The development of an organizational feedback culture gets started in the management team. The previous instructions also suit very well for the development of the management team. Read through your leadership feedback together in the team, and take the first group dialogue of the feedback of your CEO or team leader.

The Stellar Team and each one of its members have a desire for feedback. Feedback is vital for a learning team. The attitude to evaluations and feedback is openly curious in advanced management teams. Just once more:

360s and other feedback reports are primarily a tool for a dialogue, nothing more

It does not, in itself, benefit anyone, whether an average in some competence area is 3.5 or 3.9. It is certainly nice to know, but after the experience of hundreds of management evaluations we can state that the same yearning is repeated every time: „More open responses!%Why so? In open responses you can better hear the personal voice of individuals and you hear clearly understandable feedback. So why not spend time and energy on taking the reports into real use with open dialogue!

WAKE UP! IF YOU HAD AN ADVANCED FEEDBACK CULTURE, NO 360 DEGREE EVALUATIONS WOULD BE NECESSARY.

FEEDBACK MUST BE GIVEN IMMEDIATELY AND DIRECTLY TO THE PERSON(S) CONCERNED, EYE TO EYE, IN AREAS WHERE THEY ARE GOOD, AS WELL AS IN AREAS WHERE THEY NEED IMPROVEMENT. ALL YEAR ROUND.

"I will give feedback at the appropriate moment" – *Incorrect!*

An appropriate moment never comes. You only need to take yourself by the scruff of the neck and decide to give feedback. You need a desire to put effort into developing your feedback skills and a sufficient proportion of self-efficacy. Where do you get that self-efficacy from?

The concept of self-efficacy was created by the Canadian psychologist Albert Bandura. In the 1990s, after long-term research, he created a theory of self-efficacy, which means the individual's belief in personal ability to influence his/her own life. Self-efficacy has a significant influence on the choices people make and on how persistently they strive to overcome adversities.

Self-efficacy is an important success factor in feedback practice. The more you feel you are able to influence your management team and its culture, the more you will use feedback as a method for influencing. Being able to give feedback requires the experience of self-efficacy. Fortunately, self-efficacy is not in the genes but, as the research shows, it can be exercised. Self-efficacy is empowered when you overcome your internal obstacles and you try, even though you cannot be sure of the end result. Success feeds success, and in this way every moment becomes an appropriate moment for feedback. Being a living example of this, you will certainly affect the feedback culture of your team. In an advanced feedback culture, you are able to give feedback immediately to whomever it may concern. Every day and all year round.

Asking for feedback takes courage

„All is well as long as they are quiet and seem to be satisfied . . .‰ Incorrect!

Feedback is challenging, and as the feedback situation comes closer, it leads the human mind into performing its own tricks. It builds excuses to avoid uncomfortable situations. Our daily life can even be so hectic that asking for feedback often feels worthless as you have more important things to do. A typical thinking bias is connected to the recognized silence in our claim above. If nobody talks spontaneously and gives feedback, it means automatically that all is well. We believe that if there were problems or reasons to complain, people would come and tell us.

In a Stellar Team, feedback is continuously asked for. It can be asked for concerning a certain area, where an individual requires feedback from others. For example, in an upcoming presentation it might focus on clarity of communication, function of argumentation, credibility, or even on the unintentional use of euphemisms. When feedback is asked for concerning a certain area, it will be easier to direct the observations and also the feedback to that required area. You get what you ask for! In an advanced feedback culture, silence is not feedback but real feedback is asked for continuously, throughout the year.

Acknowledging feedback requires consideration

„Reaction on feedback must be genuinely intuitive‰ Incorrect!

Successfully given feedback has an influence on the person receiving it. It offers a unique opportunity to see the world with new eyes. Feedback makes most of us react immediately, before any thinking starts. Our mouths open and offer needless stuff, which are called defences. We have a need to explain, to defend, to ignore, or to hit back. You are wrong; I am right.

The human apparatus is constructed in such a way that we learn in the first couple of decades, in our childhood home with our families, a certain way to give, to ask for and particularly to receive feedback. Those who have had a learning environment, which offered sufficient safety and acceptance, will not need to defend themselves as adults. You can be yourself and the feedback offered only tells you what has already happened. You cannot change what has happened, but it is relevant to deal with it for the future. Respectively those who have received in their mother's milk, or in struggling for it, the need to defend, will take up a defensive position also later on. A quick and especially a defensive reaction reveals part of an individual's history of interaction. At the same time it communicates that at this moment the circumstances are not safe enough for him/her to enable the reception of feedback in a calm manner. By demonstrating such a quick reaction the person may imagine that he or she is saving face. The opportunity to learn has already been lost.

In a Stellar Team receiving feedback receives special attention. As we learn how to give feedback, its influence becomes clearer. If a defensive reaction in receiving feedback is noticeable inside the team, you must give feedback about this too. When you develop a feedback culture in your team where you can give feedback on feedback, the wings of feedback will really take you high. The more open feedback culture you build in your management team, the better feedback will be transformed from a threat into an opportunity.

Feedback skills are the wings of development! In an advanced feedback culture feedback is given and received eye to eye. For better for worse, all year round.

12 Collaboration is a choice

POSITIVITY INTOLERANCE

Symptoms: Discouraging negativity and tragicomic pursuit of truth

Positivity intolerance is a general phenomenon in many Nordic cultures, but in the toughest management teams it has developed into so called *yummy-yummy allergy*. Even a minuscule portion of praise or positivity causes pimples to an allergic person. The starting point for this disease is a morbid pursuit of realism. In the background there is often an underlying tendency towards perfectionism and being straightforward, which are called honesty by the patient.

A *yummy-yummy allergic* management team generally sets the goals high. If the goal is not achieved, the result is unambiguously „poor‰ and the members donÊ even try to say anything positive about it. If the goal is reached or even exceeded, they state: the result is in line with the goal. Strongly influenced by alcohol, someone may slip in a hyper exaggerating expression „not bad‰ but the state will very soon change to honest hangover.

Positivity intolerance often develops an additional discomfort, so-called *fault eye*. The patient finds faults and mistakes all the time and everywhere. The patient may be secretly even proud of this ability to find quality defects (but not too proud). The worst pain for a patient with *positivity intolerance* is praise without reason – and the only reasonable praise are comments like „the deceased was a good man in life‰ This kind of communication discourages and saddens a normal, living human being. *Yummy-yummy allergic people* put dampers on the enthusiasm and productivity of the healthy.

Care instructions in Appendix 2: ÅSelf care guide for management teamsÊ

A management team is about collaborative relationships. This may sound soft, and that is why our next question is interesting: How do we make these relationships produce good cooperation and hard results? What do we mean by collaboration skills?

Our last area of Primary Goals directs our minds to the energy in a team and to the means that make development and learning come true in a team. Becoming a learning management team materializes through conscious choices. With collaboration and learning together in mind, we will explore the underlying approaches and the ways of thinking and acting, which are linked partially directly, partially indirectly to the daily work of a management team. Our first choice is positive.

Positive psychology supports the Stellar Team

Positive psychology is a branch of psychology that focuses on human well-being, strengths and resources, as well as on their promotion. This part of psychology was virtually forgotten as World War II trauma patientsÊneeds outstripped all resources, and it only resurfaced again at the end of 1990s. Positive psychology started a determined search for information on what makes life worth living. Internationally, one of the most famous advocates of positive psychology is Martin Seligman, Professor of Psychology at the University of Pennsylvania.

Since the beginning of the millennium, there have been thousands of published „studies of happiness‰which consist of, for instance, practical information on the connection between mood and success.

Here is an example, told by Dr Seligman:
A school class was divided into three equally talented groups for a test in mathematics. Group 1 performed the test immediately. In Group 2, everyone got, surprisingly, a piece of chocolate before the start of the test. Group 3 was first asked to remember a happy event when the student had been jumping for joy. Group 2 and Group 3 performed the test with better scores than Group 1.
– But this hardly applies to us grown ups, who have a more developed brain, a controlled nature, and whose math challenges are at management team level. . .

Many other researchers have also identified the significance of mood in human behaviour.

- People who experience pleasant emotions are more flexible, creative, cooperative and open to new information, as well as efficient in their thinking (Isen 2000).
- The quantity ratio of positive and negative communication influences the quality of human relations, the cohesion of a team, decision-making and success in social structures (Fredrickson and Losada 2005).

- Positive emotions add flexibility and increase coping in occasional adversities (Fredrickson 2006).

WAKE UP! THESE STUDIES ARE NOT ONLY "NICE TO KNOW", THEY MUST BE APPLIED TO THE ROUTINES OF MANAGEMENT TEAMS. LOOK INTO THE MIRROR AND RESPOND HONESTLY: HOW DO I CREATE POSITIVE ATMOSPHERE IN OUR TEAM?

A change in attitude may have very far-reaching consequences. In a study of nuns and their attitude to life, it was found that the nuns with a positive attitude lived up to 10 years longer than the negative ones. Just for the sake of comparison: the life expectancy of non-smokers and smokers differs only 3.5 years in favour of non-smokers.

Positive psychology in the cockpit

Martin Seligman presents in his book *Flourish* (2011) a model called *PERMA*, which consists of five basic elements of a good life:

Positive emotions
Engagement
Relationships
Meaning
Accomplishment

These five researched factors bring flourishing into the daily work of the management team, because they inevitably influence the productivity of collaboration. Or what would you think, if the following perceptions were made about each member of your team?

- **Positive emotions** – We donĥt need to be satisfied or happy all the time; but HOW ABOUT, quite often, showing your joy, enthusiasm, pride, gratitude for any reason. . .?
- **Engagement** – Our work may be quite tough and family life on the side moderately demanding, but HOW ABOUT, quite often, expressing your full commitment to your role as management team member, taking total responsibility for the safety of your family in all circumstances, taking care of your personal wellbeing and your important relaxation and rest. . .?
- **Important relationships** – Most of our time goes to work and concentrating on our duties; but HOW ABOUT, quite often, communicating your appreciation to your important colleagues, your beloved family, your closest relatives, your best friends. . .?
- **Meaning** – Our work may sometimes be confusing and, upon closer inspection, many moments of our lives may seem meaningless; but HOW ABOUT, quite often, stating that exactly this job offers meaning to yourself

and this job has a meaning for other people, and your whole life may have significant meaning for some people, just because of your small, positive acts. . .?

- **Accomplishment** – Our productive results may often be very abstract and our goals seem very distant; but HOW ABOUT, quite often, just stopping to sigh: again, I took one step ahead, one item ticked off on my to-do-list, a milestone reached, a commitment fulfilled, again a stage finished. . .?

While directing attention to those five phenomena and doing – quite often – things that are listed there, all of us will reach in our lives a state that Martin Seligman calls *human flourishing*. Studies in positive psychology show that positive emotions are contagious. When you give flourishing a chance, it will catch on also in your management team, even across tables that are 10 feet wide!

WAKE UP! BE NOW SOMEONE! YOU ARE THE MEMBER IN A MANAGEMENT TEAM WHERE SOMEONE ALWAYS SHOWS POSITIVE EMOTIONS, EXPRESSES COMMITMENT, COMMUNICATES IMPORTANT RELATIONSHIPS, STATES THE MEANINGFULNESS OF YOUR MANAGEMENT TEAM AND IS HAPPY WITH ITS ACCOMPLISHMENTS.

Management team is milking and being milked

Happiness and its positive impacts on the results of work have been studied with dairy cows in the 1960s. After that the same has been repeated in a number of human studies. The factors that add to job satisfaction and happiness (and dairy litres) the most, are surprisingly not cool background music, a free cola machine and a nice boss. Combining a number of studies, we can conclude that people (including management teams) are amazingly demanding – the most important factors are the following.

- I do what I am good at – In other words I feel I control the challenges of my job, I know how to do my job, so I succeed often in it and I can perceive positive feedback.
- I do what I like – I have myself chosen to stay in this job, this job gives me pleasure, it is congruent with my values.
- I do what is beneficial for my organization – I promote, support and assist the operations of my organization, my action influences others, my job has a meaning.

Most likely every job has temporarily moments and stages which do not meet the above mentioned criteria. If your job, however, includes those elements predominantly and you remind yourself of them, you will make your brain achieve what it is capable of doing, at its best.

QUESTIONS: Ask yourself and your colleagues

1. How much do you do what you are good at? 2. How much do you do what you like? 3. How much do you do that is beneficial for your organizations? Compare your evaluations and make conclusions. . .

A couple of hints on helping yourself and others too.

- Cynicism and sarcasm influence people unconsciously – avoid them consciously, tell people instead why you are happy, excited, proud, grateful . . .
- Continuous use of weak characteristics and learned strengths is exhausting – guide people to use authentic strengths!
  Finding latent strengths and applying identified strengths is inspiring and energizing – guide people to find and apply them!
- Positivity is more important than happiness – guide people to experience pleasant emotions! (For example, the most pleasant emotions are joy, happiness, contentment, gratitude, cohesion, peace, enthusiasm, serenity, love, survival, self-efficacy, being good enough, success . . . What pleases you?)

Appreciative approach inspires

Every one of us has experienced how authentic appreciation causes a very positive emotion, and the emotion gets stronger the more valued the person is who is appreciating you. The positive emotion is even stronger when the appreciation comes from a group of people, instead of an individual. Inspired by the significant influence of positive emotions, Americans David Cooperrider and Suresh Srivastva developed a combination of methods and thinking models, which they named Appreciative Inquiry (Cooperrider and Srivastva 1987).

Appreciative Inquiry is used in many applications for organizational development, personal reviews and team workshops, for instance. The goal is to make the interviewed person aware of his or her success and skills, and then strengthen the impression in order to inspire that person to develop his/her skills further and to succeed even more. In a management team this method can be utilized to open a meeting and to create a positive and productive atmosphere.

Stages of Appreciative Inquiry in a team

1. We appreciate what we already have – we find situations of excellence and success.
2. We visualize, what could be – we create a dream of an ideal situation in the future.

3.   We create in a dialogue on what should be – we plan new structures and modus operandi.
4.   We innovate on how to reach the future – we make an action plan to implement the dream.

TRY THIS: Appreciative Inspiring!

Ask your colleague the following questions and observe how he or she changes during the interview:

1.   Tell me about a top moment in your work – it can be a small and quickly experienced situation or success in a big task, which inspired and delighted you so you were proud of your success and you wanted more of this kind of situation in your work.

    –   Tell me first briefly what this top moment was about.
    –   Tell me now more precisely about your top moment.
    –   Describe this top moment in detail and precisely, stage by stage.
    –   What made it a top moment?
    –   What did you do in that situation? How did you make this top moment possible?
    –   Which of your skills did you use? How have you acquired these skills?
    –   What did the others do, how did your working community enable your success?

2.   Future development

    –   How will you notice in the future that these skills of yours have become even stronger and that you will be able to act even better, if you want to?
    –   What kind of things are going to happen then?
    –   How have you enabled that development?

Common reflection and three levels of learning

The aim of Appreciative Inquiry and all other models of permissive asking is to provoke the use of Deep Analysis and to reflect on our own action. Reflection is necessary for learning for individuals and organizations. In active reflection, the attention of an individual or a group is directed towards handling the action and experiences. What happened? What did I observe, feel or learn? What did we observe, feel or learn?

Being aware of models of thinking or decision-making, and questioning them, is very important for the capability of individual or organizational learning.

Reflection can be done alone but in general productive reflection from different perspectives requires interaction with others. When a management team learns how to do it together, the prerequisites to become a Stellar Team grow.

Reflection and learning in a management team can be reviewed in a three-level learning process, presented by Chris Argyris and Donald Schön in 1978. The first and lowest level is the so-called *single-loop learning*, when the learning is mostly correcting detected errors. Quality deviations are discovered, reported and corrected. On an individual level you notice your own failures, which you correct as soon as possible. Changing modus operandi does not mean on this level that knowledge or understanding have altered.

Double-loop learning represents a deeper level of learning where a management team changes its conceptions, beliefs and norms in its modus operandi and culture. In this way, the learning generates much more sustainable elements in the operations.

The second level learning in management teams means that the team detects disadvantages because the operating conditions have changed due to an evolving market situation. The second level learning appears also at mind-set level which results in changes of attitude and operations in the team. An example of this is a management team which renewed its reward model and ended up instituting a common incentive instead of an individual model.

Triple-loop learning processes increase common awareness in the management team. At this third level the team is able to take some distance from its actions and its interest in how to learn as a team. It is also called meta-learning or the ability to learn how to learn. Here the management team uses its time to reflect on its learning ability.

Simplified, the third level in management teams means that the team stops regularly to evaluate its learning.

A management team in a sales organization decided to invest their time in a quarterly mutual learning discussion, as a part of their management team meeting. They booked half an hour for this retrospective, which was guided by the following questions:

- *What have we accomplished together? Where have we succeeded?*
- *Which factors have enabled our success? Which activities would have made the success even greater?*
- *How did we act as a team? What feedback do we give ourselves on our team action? Where have we improved? Where do we need to improve in the next quarter?*

The third level learning becomes real, specifically with the last set of questions. When a management team takes a regular evaluation on its agenda, the development will become established as a part of the team culture.

Figure PS.III Star Goals

Core of Part III: the attraction of Primary Goals

This book takes you on a metaphorical journey to the stars. We develop your management team into a Stellar Team, which will raise its operations up to a new level in results. In Part III we took a look at the Primary Goals of a management team; they form the attractive core of the guiding star for our development journey. Primary Goals lead us to learning, and also onto important insights and questions.

• A Stellar Team is committed. What guides and rewards this team? Which commitments make us a Stellar Team?
• A Stellar Team chooses to trust. What is our mutual trust based on? How do we nourish and strengthen it?
• A Stellar Team lives and grows from feedback. How do we develop a new feedback culture, in which we give, ask for and receive feedback – every day, all year round?
• A Stellar Team collaborates efficiently, it learns and develops constantly. How do we use positive psychology, the benefit of spontaneity and express appreciation?
• Stellar Team members know how to set common goals, they see colleagues as potential for success and they influence primarily by asking questions.
• The daily work of a successful Stellar Team is formed of chains of thinking–desiring–acting. A Stellar Team is able to support right thinking, which is followed by right acting. When a management team does this systematically,

it changes both the culture of co-operation in the organization and the results. The Stellar Team ascends, thanks to its membersÊco-operation, up to a new level of results!

It is important to remember that the Primary Goals are NOT an end in themselves. A Stellar Team needs to reach a sufficiently functioning level in the secondary area, in order to generate real results with our efforts on the primary area. Focusing clearly on team operations and on the psychologist-sounding dynamics of collaboration or other primary area reflections will not lead to any desired results, unless the development efforts are closely connected to the issues in the secondary area. Primary and Secondary Goals are like the chicken and the egg. Both are equally needed for common learning and development!

Part IV

To the stars

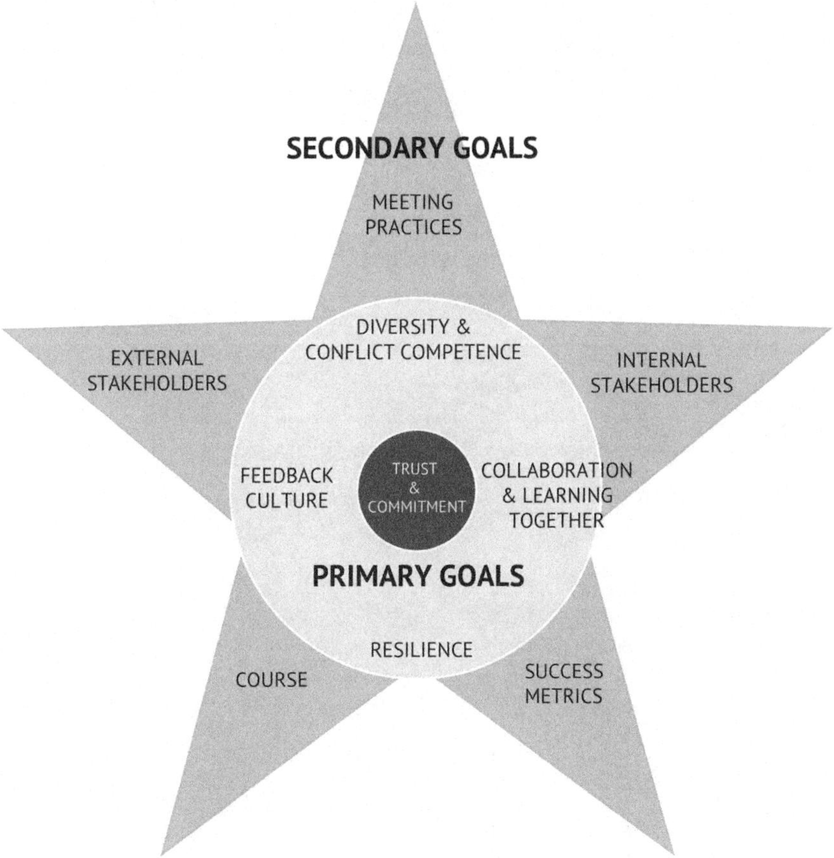

Figure PIV.1 Star Goals

13 Hey, we are airborne!

MANAGEMENT TEAM OEDEMA

Symptoms: Stiffness in decision-making and dreariness of interaction

Management team oedema (swelling) is a rather common disease. It has its roots in thoughtlessness and sheer goodness, which lead to a tendency to form the widest possible group of decision makers, representing all the different parts of the organization. The *swelling* is very easy to diagnose – like counting the fingers on one hand. Namely, the initial symptoms appear when the management team has more than seven members. If the group size goes over ten, *management team oedema* becomes a serious problem. Activities slow down, decision-making becomes stiff and going through the agenda only makes a scratch on the surface.

Care instructions in Appendix 2: ÅSelf care guide for management teamsÊ

The foundation of a Stellar Team has now been created. The launch pad or the Secondary Goals are in place, and the attraction factors, i.e. the Primary Goals, bring the necessary lifting force to the movement and ensure an inspiring journey toward the guiding star. On our way, however, we still need a variety of skills to support the team in agile reactions. A certain expertise is required from the team and another type from its captain. Additionally, in this section we address a number of aspects, where we look at both individual and group level methods of influencing, in order to ensure that the team stays on the right track. We also dig deeper in change ability and resilience, because it is those skills that enable us to overcome surprises that will guarantee us a successful journey.

We know theoretically a lot, but that is not enough – we have to know how to act in practice. When the common flight is boosted by the understanding of roles and their use, the speed accelerates. Change of role can be compared to change of thinking hats, and lots of those hats are needed in a skilful management team. In the end, it is all about the right people changing hats – and the team will develop, when everyone develops themselves, sometimes assisted by an external team coach.

Right people in right places

The right action of a management team is based on people acting in the right way. When we build a really good management team, the ideal goal is to choose the right members, however a realistic goal is that the existing members will develop their modus operandi. The quality of the team is crucial and it is measured in its critical capability to control the implementation of the basic task in the strategy. Quality is generated by members who complement each other and create synergy that results in more than the sum of its parts. The right people are those who want to grow to their real size as human beings without delay.

JUST A MINUTE: What kind of colleagues do you have around you?

How do you produce inspiration and energy in them? Would each one of them be more like the „right%team members, if they had more inspiration and energy? Or is it, in your opinion, just a matter of not directing their enthusiasm correctly? How can you help those people to try a different leadership role (more suitable for your ideals, perhaps)? Or is there possibly some need to widen your own leadership know-how?

What's inside the hat of a real leader?

The members of the highest level management team are often directors of business functions or business units. Thus, all of them already are wearing a „directorŝ hat‰ which obliges them to keep their own team of subordinates in shape. Membership of a management team gives them another type of „directorŝ hat‰that of the role of management team member. This hat contains the obligation to produce collective inspiration and energy even in colleagues. Both hats require strong leadership.

We know from experience that a director must sometimes decide quickly, make a decision instinctively out of the „hat‰ in other words with Hasty Intuition.

Herbert Simon has researched chess masters and has come to the conclusion that a master sees the setting on the chessboard differently than a beginner. A beginner may start with an intuitive move, but that move comes from a hat, which is fairly empty. An expert sees the game and connects it to perhaps thousands of experiences in his or her memory, and quickly produces a smart move from a full hat. That is real know-how.

A good hat of a director or a management team member is filled with real data and expertise, and that means that this good hat contains the intuition of an expert. When this director also has leadership as his or her own expertise, the combination becomes invincible.

WAKE UP! THE RIGHT MEMBERS OF MANAGEMENT TEAM DEVELOP THEM-SELVES AS LEADERS. THEY ACQUIRE INFORMATION, THEY ENHANCE THEIR LEADERSHIP SKILLS AND THEY SUPPORT COLLECTIVE LEADERSHIP. THIS IS FILLING THEIR HATS! – AND ABOVE ALL, IN A STELLAR TEAM YOU CAN ACCEPT AN ANSWER EVEN FROM THE HAT OF YOUR COLLEAGUE.

Speed to fly from role diversity

So far we have spoken only metaphorically about the hats of management team members. A more theoretical concept for the same phenomenon is a *role*, which was described almost 100 years ago by Jacob Levy Moreno, the pioneer of social psychology. His approach to role theory offers a practical tool for management team members to study and develop their own ways of acting. We explore first the background theory of roles.

Roles are a concept of interaction

In social psychology the concept of role is connected to interaction. A role is situational and it depends on with whom you are interacting. Roles describe behaviour in interaction, and their diversity is immeasurable. At work you can find bumpers, withdrawers, scouts, miracle men, hedonists, seers, inquisitors, pettifoggers, patrons, cheerleaders, fools, sceptics, analysts and workers – a variety of roles that describe ways to interact in a group or in a bilateral discussion. These roles describe our behaviour and Moreno (1964) calls them *psychodramatic roles*.

Besides the psychodramatic role, the concept of *social role* is important to the members of the Stellar Team. By social role Moreno means a more general, context specific or family connected role. Social roles include, among others, management team member, manager, expert, neighbour or even spouse. When we change social roles, behaviour too will change

Moreno could say to the members of a management team: „*When you are in the social role of a management team member, you will display certain characteristics that become visible due to the influence of the other members. The members in a team influence you and how you express yourself‰*

When you move to another social role, e.g. supervisor or director, and you discuss with your own team, you reveal new aspects of yourself. You display different behaviours: you as management team member and you as supervisor. If you donÊ believe it yet, think about your social role as spouse for instance. How do you behave with your spouse? Consequently, your behaviour is changed, depending on which social role you are in.

The ability to take a role varies subject to situation, and acting in a certain role is more natural than in another. As a director, certain roles are emphasized, and respectively some roles become visible very seldom. You must for instance pounce on discrepancies between people (pouncer), lead the team towards a common goal (trailblazer) or treat each team member as an individual (treater). If taking a certain psychic role is easy for you, Moreno calls it a *well developed* role. If you have difficulties to move to another psychodramatic role, that is known as an *under developed* role. A certain role can be also *over developed* and then you notice you are acting constantly in the same role and you are missing the ability to modify your action.

> Role can be defined as the actual and tangible forms which the self takes . . .
> the functioning form the individual assumes in reacting to a specific situation
> in which other persons or objects are involved.
>
> (Moreno 1977)

This is important to us all: roles can be developed. An underdeveloped role evolves and develops, if you put effort into taking that role. You need role exercise. This makes it easier to take a role and it becomes a natural part of daily interaction.

Roles and counter roles are dancing together

Every psychodramatic role has a *counter* role. Role and counter role are inseparable, as a role does not exist without its counter role. In an interaction system the roles are in an on-going dialogue, each psychodramatic role activates an appropriate counter role in the other person. A bulldozer-type has a counter role of weathercock whilst the questioner has the explainer. The role of listener awakens the counter role of teller or manipulator. When the psychodramatic role changes, the counter role will change too.

A role can be understood through its counter role. Situations in a management team reveal how individual reactions influence the interaction system of the management team. What kind of roles do you see in your team? What are the most typical psychodramatic roles?

Applying role thinking for growth in your role requires awareness of your roles. Your behaviour is a reflection of your psychodramatic roles. Increased understanding enables strengthening of your own role as influencer. The more versatile selection of psychodramatic roles you have, the more you will have flexibility in your action in the management team – and you can change your psychodramatic role if necessary.

A growing awareness of roles requires the naming of roles. Roles typically describe action, they are doers constructed of verbs with ending -er. Questioner, bridge builder or inspirer. Psychodramatic roles can also be described with symbols or metaphors. Someone must sometimes be a policeman or a miracle maker in the management team.

CAST YOURSELF IN ROLES

1. Think of yourself in the role of management team member. See yourself as a fly on the ceiling of your meeting room. What kind of psychodramatic roles do you see yourself taking in your role? What kind of characteristics will you expose?
2. Make a list of the roles you have named. It can be a doer, a symbol or a metaphor. For example a slasher or a challenger.
3. Complete the role with an adjective describing the quality of the role. Answer the question how you act in this role. For example as a systematic slasher or as an insecure challenger.
4. Pick one or two roles that are the most typical for you and respectively one or two roles that appear only seldom.
5. Draw your conclusions on your roles. What ideas are rising up now? What are you happy with? Which roles do you miss? Which role should be subdued a little?
6. Choose a role, which you want to change. What would successful role taking in a management team meeting look like from a flyîs perspective? In which situations would that role be visible in particular?
7. Make a decision to strengthen the chosen role. How will you make sure that the role will be visible? Which one of your colleagues could give you feedback on your success?

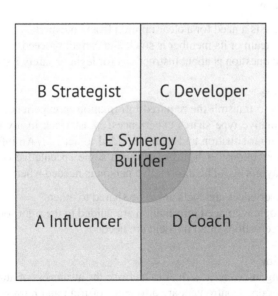

Figure 13.1 The role chart of the member of a Stellar Team: A Influencer, B Strategist, C Developer, D Coach, E Synergy builder

Role chart of a Stellar Team member

We have collected typical psychodramatic roles that are expected from the members in a Stellar Team. They form a role chart for a management team. The role chart is constructed from five main roles (Figure 13.1).

A. Influencer

Every member of a management team is basically a professional influencer. Managerial work includes a lot of situations in which influencer know-how is needed. When the management team meets, the same individual know-how should be at the use of the team. The wider spectre of know-how each team member has, the better they can adapt their actions to the situation and support the action leading to the common goal.

John Heron's *Six Categories of Intervention* offers interesting perspectives on influencing (Heron 1975). The categories of intervention are divided into two main categories, authoritative and facilitative, both of them having three different styles of influencing.

Authoritative styles proceed in a straightforward manner:

Prescriptive

A prescriptive intervention style strives to direct the behaviour of others very openly. The prescriptive style is a role of an expert who tells what others must do. This style is very natural for medical doctors, who need to tell their patients which medicine to take and how often. A prescriptive person is needed when

- there is a need for a clear opinion from an expert
- the team or its member is stuck and cannot proceed
- the question is about instructions for legal or safety issues

Informative

The aim is to transmit the required information or experience to the others. The informative type shares experiences: „Last week in my team meeting I had a similar situation and then I decided to act . . %An informative also shares observations: „I heard over lunch some speculative conversation of possible layoffs . . %The informative person is needed when

- experiences and facts are to be shared to others
- people who need information are guided to the right sources
- observations of an incident are needed.

Confronting

Confronting intervention strives to increase the awareness of attitudes, talking and behaviours. Confronters are advocates of truth and mirrors reflecting all their observations and feedback: „I have told you this already four times. I just wonder why this doesnê progress?%A confronting person is needed when

- provocation, new thinking or action is required
- an individual or a team is guided to develop and to move into their discomfort zone
- you want to give constructive feedback.

Facilitative styles influence more indirectly.

Cathartic
Cathartic intervention strives to create circumstances where the other can express himself/herself on an emotional level. If emotions are stifled there will be no space for creativity. People with the cathartic style may use themselves and their own ability to identify emotions: „I am confused and a little bit lost. How about you?%The cathartic knows how to offer interpretations on an emotional level: „I have noticed that always when you talk about issue X you look anxious. Do you notice that?%The cathartic person is needed when

- the others are frustrated or irritated
- there is dissatisfaction and lack of inspiration in the team
- there is fear of failure or a deficit in self-esteem within a team.

Catalytic
Catalytic intervention offers the others methods for the reflection and exploration of an issue together. Catalytic types open doors for widening thinking and acquiring more understanding. The catalytic says simply: „That was interesting, tell me more . . %They can also say: „Tell me, how did you act last time with that problematic guy in your team. How did you make that work?%A catalytic person is needed when

- common understanding needs to be deepened
- taking responsibility needs to be encouraged
- the commitment of the team must be increased.

Supportive
Supportive intervention directs the focus of attention to the other person with an accepting and empowering approach. A supportive person might say: „That was really an important point of view. I can see how much success in this case means to you!%A supportive person is needed when

- self-confidence of an individual or a team is to be strengthened
- a supportive culture is being created in a team
- people are being guided towards risk taking.

B. Strategist

The role of a strategist requires many kinds of skills in order to keep the journey advancing on to the stars. „*There are rule takers, rule breakers and rule makers‰* Every member of a Stellar Team must be able to play in different roles. The strategist is an *implementer* of strategy, who chunks down the strategy into daily operations, as well as inspiringly distributing tasks. This role also ensures the result and takes care that the team keeps on moving towards a goal. The strategist sees the whole and looks at the opportunities for the future. Expressing opinions actively and making proposals to the team is typical in this role. The strategist also has the ability to inspire others to think in a new way. The strategist focuses on the essentials and takes care of staying on track and not digressing from the current topic.

C. Developer

In the role of developer the management team member takes responsibility for common operations and collaboration. The developer not only represents his or her own unit but is also more interested in common development needs. This role gives a good example: personal ambition in learning underlies the pursuit of continuous development. The developer takes responsibility for common development and finishes the agreed projects categorically. Developers live from feedback, they want to give and receive feedback – constantly. They also have an exceptional ability to make observations on team operations, which they actively present to others.

D. Coach

The coach is one of the key roles in a Stellar Team. The philosophy of coaching is based on the skill of making stars of others. Attention is primarily on colleagues. This means interest in othersÊthinking and know-how concerning dialogue. The more there is a coaching approach in the management team, the more flexibly the different perspectives and competences of the team will come into common use. Coaches show their interest in others and inspire them with their encouraging attitude. Coaches see opportunities and possibilities in others, and they are also capable of giving constructive feedback to their colleagues. Additionally, they make effective questions that promote internal discussion in the team.

E. Synergy builder

A synergy builder in a management team directs attention to collaboration and its development. They are wholeheartedly in the team and they activate other members to collaborate. Synergy builders implement agreed steps and they know how important it is to repeat things: when you take one step and repeat it enough, you can reach any destination. Synergy builders value diversity in the team and this shows in their behaviour.

Captain of the team

The role chart of the Stellar Team describes, on an individual level, the forms of behaviour that are necessary in a successful management team. Additionally, most members have their own management responsibilities in their own teams or units, as well as their competences in substance know-how areas.

When a member of a Stellar Team is acting in a management team, he or she is, according to theories, in the social role of *management team member*. When he or she leaves the meeting room, the social role changes. That member becomes *director* or *expert* of a certain area. Those roles are naturally different from that of management team member. Without any deeper specification of the director̂s mind-set, the most important thing for the Stellar Team is that all members apply similar modus operandi in their managerial roles as their colleagues do.

A management team member can never take his hat off

The management team emits different types of messages to the other parts of the organization and these create an image of unity (or disagreement) within the team. It is not uncommon that management team members are not always capable of bearing their responsibility as a team member outside their team meetings.

> *The management team of a midsize industrial enterprise was split in two. The old fellows had been representing the company for 10 years, while the younger had joined only a couple of years ago. There were seven members in the management team and the balance was 4–3 in favour of the old ones. The CEO had joined the company some years ago and he had started wondering about the rumours of incompetence of new team members. There was also talk about a competence bias in the management team, as some more traditional parts of the organization were not represented at all.*
>
> *The CEO started a clarification with external support and found out that three of the four „old ones‰ had been spreading suspicion in their own ways and within their own teams. Some of their messages were on a very personal level. Also the CEO had received his share of the muck – after all, it was he who had chosen his team.*
>
> *The management team members had not behaved according to the requirements of their roles, and this had consequences. The entire organization was in a state of uncertainty.*

The membership of the management team is a 24/7 obligation. When the role changes, the hat of the management team member stays on your head, in any situation. The hats, however, become easily mixed if the foundation of the management team is not right. If there are internal tensions and an inability to deal with issues that eat away at collaboration, the internal infection will drain out and the team members begin talking maliciously about their colleagues.

Disagreement poisons the system

Another difficulty in changing the role is connected to the disability of controlling one's own emotional reactions outside the management team. When a member of the management team moves in to the working community, he or she always represents the voice of the management team – it doesn't depend on his or her own will.

Birgit was the CEO of an organization with a couple of hundreds of employees. She was regarded as a determined leader with strong opinions on many issues. Johan, the development manager, was one of the driving forces in her team. He had been hired to renew the organization and had even succeeded in many ways. Birgit was, however, forced to seize upon Johan's action in the working community, because Johan had a tendency to play solo and openly tell his own opinions, which went against the common instructions of the management team. When Birgit raised the issue with Johan, he began to realize the consequences of his action. Particularly influential in Birgit's feedback was the information that the members of the working community had started wondering about the contradictory behaviour of the management team members.

The role of management team member lives strongly even outside the meeting room. The role never disappears entirely. The other members of the organization observe management team members under a magnifying glass and even unconsciously they make interpretations about all verbal and non-verbal messages.

Birgit and Johan agreed on common rules, first together and later with others in the team. The ground rules ensured the appropriate unity of communication outside the meetings. They ended up with the decision that possible disagreement must be handled within the team and everyone was committed a) not to pull the rug from under a colleague or b) not to visibly act against agreed guidelines under the watchful eyes of other employees of the organization.

It is self-evident that the management team deals with lots of confidential issues, which cannot be discussed with others in the organization. If emotional issues are left untreated within the team, keeping them inside your head will take a lot of energy. When there is enough trust in the team, all the emotions can be let out and even a heated debate becomes possible. When a decision is made and all the emotions have been vented, the case is closed, the meeting finishes and everybody assumes the role of supporter of collective leadership. This is a fundamental factor of success.

Birgit and Johan and all the management team made together common rules for themselves, in order to strengthen collective leadership:

1. *I will tell (only) positive gossip about my colleagues.*
2. *I will express my potential doubts, annoyances or disappointments straight to my colleagues, preferably in our meetings.*
3. *I decide not to burden the other members of the community with my excessive criticism. My duty is to support, not to shoot down anybody's ideas.*
4. *I want to support my colleagues in succeeding. I will offer assistance to others and ask for help if I need it.*

Member of a management team between a rock and a hard place

When you join a group of other employees as a member of the management team, the conversation changes. You cannot escape your role. The status remains, as do expectations related to it.

Different people have different expectations and a management team member works in permanent crossfire of expectations. This sometimes leads to unconscious choices that are perhaps not suitable for the light of day. When the expectations of subordinates, management team colleagues and your own supervisor draw in different directions, you have to prioritize and make choices. It is impossible to fulfil everybody's expectations at the same time.

Charles works as an IT manager in the pharmaceutical industry and he is a member of the management team. The team recently decided on strategic direction and planned preliminary operations, in which they would invest during the upcoming fiscal year. That meant a clear change compared to the current situation and they anticipated change resistance by employees. The management team members agreed to take care for their part that they would support the new strategy by their own example.

> *The next week Charles had a development day with his own team, and his team members began to question the new strategy. Charles at first was listening to the argumentation but he noticed that soon he was in the same conversation criticising the new strategy. The agreement with management colleagues had been overruled by the angry voices of his team.*
>
> *Charles wanted, in the first place, to meet the expectations of his own team. When he stopped to think about the different expectations, the conflict became apparent. In Figure 13.2, Charles named the expectations of his subordinates, colleagues and his supervisor. The most conflicting expectations are highlighted.*

As a management team member you can regularly be between a rock and a hard place, but you are always primarily a member of the management team. You have to be aware of different expectations. If meeting the expectations of your employee team goes before your colleagues or supervisor, you are going to be in trouble within a short time. It is impossible to bow to many directions at the same time, so you need to make choices. Choices are made with considerations of Deep Analysing, without letting momentary hijacks of emotions and needs to please take over. Sticking to the common line together in the management team is vital to implement changes!

Figure 13.2 An example of the controverting expectations of a management team member

The chair really matters

The management team members are important factors in building a Stellar Team but the chair of the team is definitely nothing less. If the others carry their responsibilities and act without blame in their roles, the chair must do the same with full effort. This is not always the case.

The CEO and other leaders of management teams mostly adapt to the existing culture and conduct. Many times the model is individual centred, so the goals are set primarily to individuals and their implementation is connected to incentives. The team leader may also think that creating a culture of internal competition will make the individuals seek constant improvement in their performance.

Sometimes we also come across hidden motives when the team leader seems to have a need to keep the members busy with their individual tasks. This ensures that they wonît have the time and energy to challenge their own supervisor. Perhaps somebody might even think that focusing on management team level goals may strengthen the team so much that it will become a threat to his or her own position of power.

In hard times many believe in tough measures. Weak leaders start to implement something they call „strong leadership‰That is instructing, commanding, controlling, monitoring. A weak leader lacks the courage to indulge in open interaction with subordinates and to delegate leadership to others. A weak leader fears losing leadership irrevocably.

The goal of the chair is not to show his or her own excellence but to enable the discussion. Successful leadership means building up a common purpose and strives to connect purpose to practice – by widely involving the management team members. The wisdom of the chair also includes an ethical dimension. Leadership is not a person nor a position, which means the question is not about the quality of the person sitting at the table or possessing the gavel. Good leadership is a complex and morality centred relationship between people, and it is based on trust, obligation, commitment, emotion, and on a shared vision of the good (Ciulla 2004).

The leader of a management team, CEO, or director of a business unit is in a significant role for showing example. The bearer of leadership understands deeper the dimensions of leadership. It is totally different „to be a leader‰than „to take leadership‰The role of a leader is a concept that is connected to the task and organizational position, but leadership is not linked to the task. Good team leaders and directors have the skill to take leadership and initiate the desire to follow.

The chair is not alone with his or her skills but the leadership is also divided among the other members of the management team. The more there are those who take leadership in the team, the higher the quality of the dance between leadership and followship will be in the management team. Thus leadership is independent of the position, but it is a phenomenon of the team interaction, in which both leadership and responsibility are shared.

A department manager in a public entity was a valued expert. He had a reputation as a top specialist in his own area. His role as a leader was not highly appreciated in the organization. He appeared to be a distant and slightly absent-minded supervisor, whose thoughts were sometimes difficult to catch hold of. In a management team training an idea popped up, which he found inspiring: each member of the management team was assigned to lead two meetings during the operational year. His obligation as official manager was to ensure that the necessary decisions were made. His strong competence in evaluation and analysis was desired to be utilized for common benefit, rather than him concentrating on leading the team meetings. Additionally he wanted to learn from other chairs how to lead meetings. At the same time all of them learned from each other, because the team agreed on common feedback practices.

PERSUADE: Rotating chair

Some teams have tried and made this a permanent practice. They say it does not matter who is the chair as long as the meetings are well prepared.
– How would your team take to a rotating chair?

Change of role must be recognized

The leader of management team has a supervisor of his or her own, and at the highest hierarchy level of an organization it is the chairman of the board. A functioning relationship between the CEO and the chairman of the board creates highly positive prerequisites to construct a Stellar Team.

The function of this collaboration is not self-evident. Unclear responsibilities of the roles cause a specific inertia in this relationship. If the CEO is also simultaneously wearing other „hats‰ the need for clarification will increase. In smaller enterprises, it is not at all unusual that the CEO is the business owner and also a member of the board. If the same person is also active in business operations, the hats easily become mixed.

Marco was a director in a family business – third generation. He owned the company together with his three sisters. Marco and his sister Miriam were both operations directors and members of the management team. Marco was the CEO and Miriam was the marketing director. Additionally, Miriam was the chair of the board. Two other sisters were only shareholders of the company.

These cross-power positions of Marco and Miriam were causing problems in the management team. It was difficult for Marco to intervene in Miriam's operations. Miriam was his big sister, direct subordinate and still his supervisor. The roles were positioned in a quite challenging way.

In the case of Marco and Miriam the key to the solution was found when the management team dared to put the cat on the table. The most remarkable comprehension gained during the process was Marcos's insight into how important it was to behave in accordance with his own role of responsibility. Changing the role changes the game!

14 Resilience prevents motion sickness

CHANGE MOTION SICKNESS

Symptom: Inappropriate action

Change motion sickness is a relatively normal affliction for many of us. It is also often described as „feeling sick‰In practice, the feeling is caused in a change journey by the bends that arrive as a disruption for our brains expecting to advance in rectilinear motion. The sickness goes away relatively soon, and depending on the bends of change, the recovery takes perhaps only a few seconds – or in the case of sensitive individuals, a few months.

Even though the disease is well known, its appearance in the management team worries the entire organization. Inappropriate action is then detected in the management team. Basically, it is presumed that the management team has planned the change journey and its road map so precisely that not a single bend will come as a surprise. However, hardly any level of planning in advance can prevent *change motion sickness* totally, even within the management team. Surprises will always come.

Care instructions in Appendix 2: Âself care guide for management teamsÊ

Change management in change

The duty of a management team is to lead the Primary and the Secondary Goals in a changing world in order to make a profit with their business or other desired results of their organization. Thus, the management team must:

1. control its own change behaviour in the changing environment, and
2. lead the changes that are – in general demanded by the changes in the environment – necessary to secure the results of the organization.

Daily routines in the business world: competitors conquer market share with new services, the economic cycle tightens finances, we have too many employees but

The Changing World
- Business environment
- Human resources
- Technologies
- Micro and macro economics
- Etc...

(The guiding star surrounded by the Milky Way)

Figure 14.1 The Changing World

too few innovators who understand new technologies, many factors have changed since we drew up our budget and now we are in the red . . . No wonder that someone in the management feels pain in the chest. Anyhow how are we going to survive the pressure brought on by change?

Glorious success requires really skilful operating in the world of change and that̂s why resilience is one of the key competences of a Stellar Team. The characteristics of the brain explain a lot of our change behaviour. In addition, people have individual features that either speed up or slow down coping with unexpected changes. There seems to be only one thing that does not change: change management stays among the top themes of training and professional literature, year after year. Why is that so?

Paths of change in the brain

Our brain has an unambiguous main task: to keep the owner of the brain alive. Evolution has steered the development of the brain by letting those carriers of brain breed more, who are the fittest in promoting survival. The owner of the brain is kept alive when the brain steers him or her to control energy and manage risks.

Controlling energy is acquiring nutrition and, on the other hand, saving energy for critical situations. Using the brain takes energy, too. Some studies show that in sedentary work the brain uses up to 20% of the total energy consumption of the body. Learning is the most energy consuming action, which in practice is the creation of new connections between nerve cells in the brain. Changes often require a conscious creation of new connections and conscious use of Deep Analysis.

How are controlling energy and risk management then linked together? Wasting energy increases the risk of getting killed. If I have used all my energy in some pointless learning, I have no energy for fighting or fleeing when the enemy strikes. At worst, I cannot even look for nourishment. In a simplified way, the brain steers us to be wary of using energy, unless it is rewarding. But because of rewards some people even learn Latin or run after a ball!

Thus, the brain is against change but not senselessly. There is actually no such thing as change resistance but there are changes that are not rewarding. Let us compare these:

1. Get a driving licence, in other words, learn the traffic rules and how to control a vehicle. OK!
2. Get a job; in other words, learn totally new things compared to your school knowledge, ways of working, collaboration etc. OK!
3. Change your job; in other words, learn totally new ways of working, new goals, new people . . . OK!
4. Get married, in other words, learn to adapt your behaviour to the expectations of another person and additionally learn new ways of working, people . . . OK.
5. Move to a new home, in other words, learn to define the location of yourself and your belongings. OK.
6. Have children, in other words, learn all that is said above plus new habits of sleeping! Well . . . OK . . .
7. Start using a new computer system for reporting traveling expenses, in other words, learn instead of your former practice, a few new clicks and ways of entering data. No way, absolutely not! What are they thinking up there in the management when they make people do this; as if there weren͡t enough work to do here already!?

The northern neighbour of the USA

What did you think when reading the heading above? Probably your Hasty Intuition produced very quickly an explicit thought „Canada‰

Learning is creating connections between the nerve cells in the brain. Knowhow is finding the connection when the learned thing or skill is needed. As a school kid, you had to repeat a piece of information until the connection was born in the brain. So, as you finally observed in your test of geography for the question „The northern neighbour of the USA?‰your brain found as if automatically the connection between your brain cells which produced the answer „Canada‰

A learned connection can be also described by the metaphor of a path. There is a path from stimulus X to thought Y. If you don͡t recognize the stimulus USA, you don͡t even find the beginning of the path, not to mention its northern neighbour at the other end of the path.

My brain is unfinished but the situation is stable

It is human to say: don͡t change me because my faults are permanent and fortunately they are not many. There is a tendency to explain ourselves as being a permanent phenomenon, especially when it comes to weaknesses: I AM like this.

WAKE UP – YOU ARE NOT! There is nothing permanent in you other than the atoms that form you, and your tendency to explain everything about yourself in a positive light.

Let us try to put it in a softer way. Your world will change if you think: I AM not like this but I THINK NOW like this.

The brain is a neuroplastic organ. That means new connections are being born all the time between the brain cells or the neurons, and their amount can be easily increased. The latest research shows that even new brain cells are being born, even in old age! The brain is shaping itself and it can be shaped. Did you know that a human being can learn throughout his or her entire life? Now you know, and as you keep repeating this, you are learning.

I think now like this – and I change my brain

An old thinking path:
*Henry hears the expression „organizational change". A path leads from the word „**change**" to the thought „**mess**". This leads on further to a series of thoughts „it will not work, always the same, useless fumbling". This is true in Henry's world of experience, based on learning from his observations. Henry easily goes down this path, every time when he thinks of the connection between a „change" and a „mess".*

A new thinking path:
Henry wants to change his thinking. The „mess" comes again to his mind as he hears the expression „organizational change". Now Henry asks himself: What would a foolish optimist think of this? Well. For instance „you don't know yet what positive things can come out of this, I may learn something, there are certainly going to be interesting outcomes". Obviously, Henry does not believe this but while thinking like this, he connects for the first time the stimulus „change" to „optimistic ideas", in other words he opens up the path between them for the first time.

Going down a path once does not obviously make it a well-beaten path. Returning to the old well-beaten path happens automatically.

Henry begins now to exercise his new thinking. In every change situation as he notices he is thinking „always the same", he repeats to himself the question: „What would a foolish optimist think about this?" Then he repeats those optimistic ideas, which he still does not believe. However, every replay connects the neurons again and makes the new path easier to go down. Henry goes on with his repeats, consciously and determinedly.

> *One day Henry hears a stimulus „there was a **change** in the schedule of this project‰Henry thinks: „Always the same – but on the other hand, this tightening may teach us something new‰Henry'ŝ brain identified at the point of the stimulus „change‰TWO paths: one leading to pessimistic and another to optimistic thoughts. Now he may choose how to think. Next, Henry'ŝ neuroplastic organ may shape itself by rewarding choices. In other words, Henry may, in theory, transform into an optimist, if choosing the optimistic path gives him positive experiences. At the same time, the path to pessimistic thinking is becoming gradually overgrown.*

In the theory of constructivism, unlearning means wiping out old knowledge to make space for the new. Brain research does not support this possibility. If you have in your brain a learned fact *President of Finland =>Halonen*, you cannot remove that connection consciously. Instead, you can create a new connection *President of Finland =>Niinistö* and additional connections *Halonen =>former*, and *Niinistö =>current*. An overgrown path is not definitively closed. If we come to the stimulus *President of Finland, before Halonen,* we can relatively easily open up a path ending with *Ahtisaari*. The brain does not need unlearning; let us provide it with updates, e.g. following natural attrition.

New paths of the change management team

What is the meaning of neuroplasticity for good collaboration in the management team, and why do we even talk about it in this book? The reasons can be found in many perspectives.

1. **Managing the change**

   – The management team manages the change; it is a transition from the current stage to goal stage, it is development, it is changing attitude to changes taking place in the environment.
   – The management team has to create new paths, to make them rewarding and to direct the organization to convert them into new highways.

2. **Leading collaboration**

   – Collaboration requires good interaction, which is promoted by awareness of the neurology of learning; it is an authentic belief: every individual is an expert in change.
   – Leading collaboration is leading thinking: thinking is followed by action, changed thinking is followed by changed action, action brings results, changed action brings new results.

3. Self-management in change

- Members of the management team are expected to have solution competence, creativity and proactivity, that is why management team members must be able to question their own paths and to learn quickly.
- A neurological approach is merciful and goal oriented, you do not need to change your thinking but create more of it; you can end-lessly create new paths, the paths can be made into highways or they can be let become overgrown, itîs your choice.
- Changing yourself is neurologically only „hard training‰ conscious repetition and observing the rewards.

Planned and unexpected change

Changes can be divided into two categories, the planned and unexpected. For example:

1. A planned change: I decide to change my TV set. I need to learn something new to be able to use the new one, but I am motivated because the new viewing experience will be rewarding.
2. An unexpected change: the computers in our organization are changed from brand A to brand B. I must learn something new to be able to use B and I am not motivated, because I was not involved in planning this change, so I have no idea of personal rewards of this change. The change evokes negative emotions in me.

Managing a change is easy, if all involved think the change is planned and thus meets their own expectations.

> *The management of a printing enterprise made a decision to change a modus operandi concerning the employees. The employees had learned the current way and their plan was to continue with it. For the management this was a planned change, but for the employees an unexpected change, which deviated from their plan. The management was wondering why it was so difficult – and then all the employees resigned. Now the management faced a real change, which was not planned but unexpected!*

A change that evokes negative emotions is obviously against plans and therefore unpredictable.

Need to control is controlling

The fear of losing control is an amazing fear. Control means the control of both physical and mental balance. Above all, it means the security of not being surprised and losing control of oneself. The opposite of security is uncertainty that creates a stressful state and causes inappropriate behaviour. At work, it may appear as aggressiveness, avoidance, passivity or strange „flocking together‰

What is control? Turn on and off the lights with the switch in your room. The lights are on or off, exactly as you control them. What is losing control? The lights go out by themselves in your room. You try to turn them on, but the switch does not work. Imagine that it is almost dark in the room and you have an important meeting with an important partner going on. How do you feel, do you have control?

How do we create control in an uncontrolled situation? Imagine that you switch the useless switch on and off in a dark room, and the others wonder confusedly if there is any use in continuing the meeting. Imagine that then you hear the voice of your colleague: „I got a message from the reception, an electric transformer was just changed and this disruption will be fixed in five minutes.‰You can imagine how the confusion fades. You can still not turn the light on with your switch, but how does it feel now? Is the situation under control?

In unexpected changes we all strive to control. How can we provide control to others? From an individual point of view, we need meaningful action and uncontrolled is far from meaningful. A management team seeks from its point of view a meaningful justification for its decision, but often forgets that the meaning is not necessarily visible to the employees of the organization at all. At worst, people only experience shit hits the fan endlessly . . .

THINK IN ADVANCE: IDEAS OF INDIRECT CONTROL

When you implement changes that others think are „unexpected‰and they cause experience of „lacking predictability‰how do you offer them indirect control? How can you share preliminary information, interim information, information about upcoming information, information that there is no information to be shared . . .?

Change causes dysfunctional behaviour – and always evokes emotions

Just any day 1 – Individual situation:
   The coffee machine did not work in the morning, traffic was totally jammed because of some accident, I came late to my meeting, the team did not accept my proposal . . .

   How is it possible that individual A goes wild on overspeed but individual B proceeds in a normal way?

Just any day 2 – Team situation:

   The beamer in the meeting room did not work, the printed version of the report had old figures, the CEO came late to the meeting, the implementation of our strategy is not advancing as planned . . .

   How is it possible that team A gives up in this situation but team B proceeds in a normal way?

The activation level of our nerve system varies. Both over-activation and under-activation lead to inappropriate, dysfunctional behaviour. When you meet an unexpected change, i.e. a phenomenon that deviates from your plans, it causes disappointment. Disappointment in your expectations and a change in your plans cause stress and negative emotions. Stress causes over-activation of the sympathetic nervous system and stress behaviour.

A stressed person behaves inappropriately and unproductively; there are phases of over-activation and under-activation, which can easily be perceived by bystanders. Can we explain this bouncing back by factors like experience or attitude? Some of us are more used to adversities, some people just do not care?

How does recovery from change take place?

Andy is going to drive to an important meeting and now he has to drive fast to be on time. Andy comes to the parking lot where he has left his car but the car has disappeared – Andy reacts:

1.   *What the –beep!*
2.   *Andy rushes to the concierge and blames him for not watching the parking lot properly.*
3.   *Andy becomes paralyzed because this always happens to him when he has an important meeting.*
4.   *Andy gets overheated, he begins to run around the parking lot looking for his car . . .*

How does recovery from a stressful state to bouncing back to appropriate action take place? You must correct either your plan or your perception, in other words, you have to see that your disappointment is unfounded.

5. a) Correcting the plan: Andy states that, on the other hand, his colleague Bert is still going to that important meeting, and at this stage of the negotiation, it is tactically better that he himself is not there.
5. b) Correcting the perception: Andy remembers that he left his car on the street, not in the parking lot! And there he finds it.

After this, Andy's action recovers to an appropriate level, as an alternative
a) he makes a call to his colleague and tells him the new plan; in alternative
b) he drives to the meeting. – What happens to Andy between stages 4 and 5.a)?

Resilience helps bouncing back

Resilience is the capability of a system – in nature or in the human brain – to
recover from a change. The Merriam-Webster web dictionary defines this as:
*the ability of something to return to its original shape after it has been pulled,
stretched, pressed, bent, etc.* A capable system can adapt to changing circumstances and develop new ways to succeed. In ecology, resilience means the characteristics that help a naturally adaptive system to recover the balance. In data
technology it means, e.g., the programmed features of a computer network that
make the network recover automatically after crashing.

Psychological resilience is defined as an individual ability to adapt to adversities and stress, without sinking into depression or getting traumatized. Hard circumstances obviously cause emotional reactions but a resilient person has a kind
of mental flexibility, recovery potential and ability to change.

Characteristics that speed up recovery from change

For a couple of decades, organizational researchers have searched for characteristics of resilience, which can be adapted to ever changing working life, and
which will help resilient individuals and organizations to cope with changes
with agility. Daryl Conner and Linda Hoopes have found in their studies very
credible and logical characteristics for recovery from unexpected changes. The
following are the fundamental characteristics of resilience – this is our adaptation as scales.

1. **Optimism – pessimism**

    Optimism: At its best, it is the ability to view a situation in a positive light
    and to see opportunities instead of threats. You see failures as learning
    experiences, and you believe that there is plenty of good in the future.

    Pessimism: At worst, I take no action because I believe I won't suc-
    ceed anyway. I believe the future will repeat the failures of the past, even
    in greater measure. I arouse in others irritation mixed with pity.

2. **Strong self-confidence – weak self-efficacy**

    Strong self-confidence: At best, you have a strong self-efficacy and trust
    in the surrounding world. You also have strong faith in your ability to
    influence.

    Weak self-efficacy: At worst, I undervalue all my skills, I do not see
    my achievements or development. I think I have always been heaved
    recklessly by the winds. I arouse in others pity mixed with irritation.

3. **Strong focus – weak priorities**

Strong focus: At best, you are always aware of priorities and directions. This can be called impulse control, which makes your action predictable and controlled. This is also the ability to focus on one issue at a time and to close your mind to untimely and disrupting stimuli.

Weak priorities: At worst, I lose my focus totally in a critical situation. I start to organize the deck chairs of the sinking Titanic. That looks scary . . .

4. **Flexible thinking – fast locking thinking**

Flexible thinking: At best, you look for options, reflect on them, explore the causalities, analyse the situation from different perspectives and take distance.

Fast locking thinking: At worst, hasty conclusions, which I cannot give up, even if they are proven to be false. This looks ridiculous, but I consider myself to be always right.

5. **Social flexibility – coping alone**

Social flexibility: At its best, insightful ability to utilize skills of others, courage to ask for and receive help. Together we are more, especially in a critical situation.

Coping alone: At worst, mistrust towards others, isolating myself with the problem. This looks like an omnipotent introvert.

6. **Organised – disorganised**

Organized: At its best, structured, systematized action, you are sharing your plans with others so they can participate.

Disorganized: At worst, an action plan with one single item: do something, but even that is hard to keep to. All my action looks like improvisation.

7. **Proactivity – risk avoidance**

Proactivity: At best, you are courageous to take action and expose yourself to new things. You try out a direction and correct it when necessary. Experimenting, never idle waiting.

Risk avoidance: At worst, I stop, standing on one foot, because taking a step may entail unknown consequences, and then it is better to wait for things to settle down. This looks like uncertain procrastination.

An engineering company, a supplier of planning services for the electronics industry, experienced a sudden crash in their order book. Their best customer had been acquired by a multinational group and the whole production was to be moved to Asia.

The management team gathered in a gloomy mood, but the CEO, being a well-known optimist, indicated immediately that this was their learning journey to the world market – or at least, to world class operation styles. A big change was coming, but they all seemed to believe that things would work out.

They stated together that the young company had a lot of ability to learn and adapt. They believed that they could affect further development like they did when they first built up that big account.

The management team members asked themselves: what was most important in this situation? Answering was easy; they had to keep the people they had trained to be users of special programmes. They had to keep to the marketing plan. They had to maintain their financial status.

They noted that everything must not be nailed down immediately. Besides prioritizing, they had to be flexible and find out what consequences this change would bring. In this particular situation, it was useful to bring in external expertise alongside their own wisdom.

The management team ended up with an action plan with five items to handle the change. It was not perfect, so they decided to update it at least weekly. They took immediate action with item number 1: Before the rumours started to spread, they had to tell their people what they were going to do . . .

Strong resilience is the sum of equally strong characteristics

The example above described the seven important characteristics of resilience. Why are they so many – would it not be sufficient to have only a couple of strong characteristics?

The characteristics of resilience are utilized in critical change situations. Changes are the unexpected situations that cause stress and trigger stress behaviour. It is first an emotional reaction, which can be aggression, depression or some other, inappropriate action. After that, we all have a tendency to utilize our strengths.

An unexpected occurrence can be just about anything; a coffee machine out of order, or being fired. There are many kinds of surprises and you cannot cope with all of them with the same strategy. The more characteristics of resilience we have in use, the better we can choose a coping strategy exactly for the unexpected situation. When we avoid overuse of our strong characteristics and give more space for the less used and weaker characteristics, we create strong resilience. The journey to the stars will continue when, in an unexpected situation, a synergistic Stellar Team combines the strengths of its members as their joint characteristic, with the sum of their resilience characteristics.

Spontaneous management team learns

We human beings implement in our daily action the things we have learned, but fortunately we have also learned to learn more. That is why we can believe that we are constantly on the way to creating something new, or that we are even in a creative state. This is easy to detect in children. Unfortunately adultsÊfear of losing face, laziness and force of habits keep many management teams on familiar tracks and their competitiveness remains weak. A skilful and courageous management team follows the situation and moves to a creative state, and it is capable of facing up to new challenges surprisingly well – spontaneously and utilizing its resilience.

The goal of spontaneity is NOT continuous quick and intuitive thinking through Hasty Intuition.

Instead, spontaneous input from different people will generate unexpected results when the team ends up with an enhancing process making use of Deep Analysis from different people.

A creative state requires the spontaneity that is courage to be imperfect. Spontaneity is also courage to tolerate the imperfect in other people. Then it does not matter if someoneÊs answer is wrong, or even given to the wrong question. Spontaneous action always evokes resistance but when management team members learn to tolerate both spontaneity and resistance, they are constructing a creative state.

1. **Spontaneity is promoted by deep understanding, which is created by expressing your own, true ideas and emotions.**

   In a Stellar Team everyone expresses their own thoughts and emotions connected to them, even at the risk of them not being liked. The thoughts are brought up constructively with those perspectives, interests and concerns that describe best oneÊs own understanding. At the same time, it is good to react visibly to the ideas, feelings and topical problems of the others.

2. **Spontaneity is promoted by security, which is built by also dealing with the embarrassing things.**

   In a Stellar Team, there can be great differences in opinion, but all issues are discussed fairly. You should create structures and practices for discussion, which make the positive treatment of different views possible.

3. **Spontaneity is promoted by permitting the not-knowing state.**

   In a Stellar Team you dare to be not-knowing and insecure, which is agreeing with the team to reflect on new perspectives, testing different options and wondering about fresh solution models. Spontaneity is born in the here and now.

4.   Spontaneity is promoted by positive person perception.

A Stellar Team has a positive person perception and values, which are based on seeing the potential in people. Actions are based on faith in potential, on positive expectations concerning one's own success and that of others, as well as on learning new things.

Change management team in urgency on a burning platform

All of us can surely remember a situation in which we have, whilst faced with extreme disaster, come unexpectedly to a solution and cleared the situation. Based on this, we must not come to a conclusion that it would be beneficial to drive to the brink of the abyss, so that we could then find a way to salvation. It is crucial to know that every year, millions of people die accidentally or sustain injuries because they come to a false solution in an emergency situation. An emergency generates a kind of a turbo effect in the human brain, and the seemingly right solution is found rapidly with Hasty Intuition, as if by itself.

Every manager has heard the exciting story of the „*Burning Platform*‰which is used by tough change managers to support the first step „*Create the Sense of Urgency*‰according to the well-known 8-step change process.

WAKE UP! COMPETENT CHANGE MANAGEMENT DOES NOT CONNECT MOR-
TAL DANGER AND RUSHING AROUND IN A HURRY TO SUCCESSFUL CHANGE.

The misinterpreted masters of change, Daryl Conner and John Kotter, also state this.

„*Burning platform*‰

Resilience guru Daryl Conner tells how he issued the story of a burning platform after the North Sea oil rig accident in 1988. The accident killed 168 people, but the biggest impression on Conner was made by a survivor, Andy Mochan. He said in a television interview that he had two choices: bake to death or jump. That was in practice either unquestionable death or jumping from the 15th floor down to the sea, where, first, being saved was uncertain, and secondly, help had to arrive absolutely within 20 minutes.

Conner observed here a connection to a good change management. A good leader demonstrates total commitment to the change programme . . .

– Even though the *to be* state is not attractive
– Because the *as is* state causes emotional distress
– And the cost of keeping up the *as is* state helps to maintain the motivation to understand the goals of the change

Many times directors complained how, unexpectedly, they were forced to do so much work in order to implement the change. Additionally, the implementation process was uncertain and the risk of poor final results was high. There were neither appropriate resources nor suitable people. Failure threatened consequences they could not afford, and that is why they had to succeed with the first jump. In the case of Andy Mochan, the jump with its uncertainties was scary, but he had to choose between certain death or possible death.

In 1992, Daryl Conner included the story of the burning platform in his book *Managing at the Speed of Change*, and the story started to spread. And interpretations too started to go wrong. Conner himself states in his blog that in most cases his story was understood correctly, but regrettably there are two bad misconceptions circulating. We have here enhanced their CORRECTED version based on his website connerpartners.com:

> „– An organization can only muster the *RIGHT* kind of commitment necessary to successfully change *EVEN* if it is *NOT* facing circumstances with catastrophic consequences such as insolvency, toppling stock value, loss of governmental approval, an unwanted takeover, failing merger, and/or collapsing market shares.
>
> – Leaders should *NOT* intentionally manipulate information or circumstances to manufacture the appearance of urgency for change when that̂s not actually the case.‰

„*Sense of urgency*‰

Change management guru, John P. Kotter is in particular known for his 8-step process for leading change. The first step, „create the sense of urgency‰ois often misinterpreted and the word *urgency* often takes the meanings of haste and hurry. Hasty Intuition forgets in its sense of urgency that the word *urgency* has many meanings: desperation, determination, importance, imperative, necessity, need; and the adjective urgent means crucial, critical, pressing, insistent, serious; but of course we may understand it as a burning urge, which must be handled right now.

The speed of change in this world is constantly accelerating, but Kotter says haste is not a natural state of being and real haste is rare. A successful change process is initiated when those involved understand that continuing in the current state is no longer possible. The change at hand is a necessity and so the action has to be taken at once. Organizations that have managed well for ages are probably in a state of some sort of complacency and the need to change is overlooked. Particularly in this situation you have to create *urgently* a sense of a *pressing necessity*.

We will use now, instead of Kotter̂s expression, our own choice *pressing necessity*, which we want to be interpreted in the right way:

– The prevailing attitude is a desire, „We want to‰
– Determination is obvious: start moving, winning, now
– People are alert, they seek for essential information for success
– In adversities people seek for efficient ways to transmit information immediately to the right people
– People come to work every day prepared for energetic collaboration

The right *pressing necessity* is born through leadership produced by people; it is not a result of successes in the past or failures in the present. Pressing necessity is not an external force, but comes from inside, as a need to move away from the old and, on the other hand, as a passion to reach towards the new.

> *An IT wholesaler was some years ago drowning in the red sea of bloody price competition along with numerous similar enterprises. The company survived, but they wanted to review their strategy. The management team went on a retreat for a couple of days.*
>
> *After the first daŷs work, sitting in the sauna, a member of the team told the others about a book, which guided to the dream of a blue ocean. The idea of having data centre and cloud services arose. At dinner, an amazing enthusiasm started to sprout: it would be something new, it would be challenging, it would require new kinds of partnerships, it would open up a new class of customer relations. The discussion went on till late night and more interesting opportunities and attractive synergies kept on bubbling up.*
>
> *In the morning the managing team was unanimous. They had to grab this new service idea at once. This card had to be played. This enthusiasm had to be utilized. This would not be easy but the strategy was totally changed. And so many other things were also changed successfully, because, after all, everything was based on a pressing necessity.*

Amygdala makes decisions on a burning platform

Brain researchers have known for a long time that in a scary situation and in highly stressful situations the amygdala hijacks control in our brain. Daniel Goleman used the expression „amygdala hijack%some 20 years ago in his book *Emotional Intelligence* (1996). However, this information about a neurological phenomenon does not seem to be included in training courses on change management, not to mention general managerial education.

An interesting example is the award granted to Nokia CEO Stephen Elop in July 2013. The *European Association of Communication Directors* granted their *European Communication Award* to Elop for promoting business communications. This is how the organizations introduced the winner: „Stephen is recognized for his direct and transparent communication style, as evinced by his by-now famous ÂBurning PlatformÊmemo.%So you can see it even this way, although some criticized Elop̂s memo, which indeed did cause damage to Nokia . . .

WAKE UP! Don't pose any threat, unless you want others to leave their brains hanging on the rack.

Each of us has been able to bring about an amygdala hijack in another person along with the consequent animal defensive reactions: fight, flight or play dead. Each management team member must know how to do it, so it never happens because of unawareness. When the defence reaction is active, no-one uses the intellectual parts of their brain.

In a threatening situation the stimulus coming from our senses passes by the thinking brain and goes straight to the amygdala in the inner brain. The amygdala in the limbic system is the part that is responsible for emotions and animal defensive reactions.

What is then a threatening situation? Burning platform, too tight schedule, negative criticism, underrating, disparagement. How is that defence reaction generated?

The amygdala reacts according to pre-set models. Sometimes that reaction may save your life, in most cases it drives you to senseless shouting, fleeing from the situation or to the symbolic closing of your ears. A threat starts the production of certain neurotransmitters in the blink of an eye. The influence of these chemicals can be stopped if you know how to identify the behavioural models. The neurotransmitters that make you bypass your brain, lose their effect in 3–6 seconds.

Preventing an amygdala hijack requires a conscious halt and strong focus. Try these alternatives if you feel your amygdala is compelling you to fight:

a) Count to ten – this may look like you are playing dead, but this gives time for chemicals to decompose.
b) Ask for help – an unexpected change of perspective influences the system and gives you time.
c) Imagine something pleasant – this requires exercise and may seem like playing dead, but even this gives time for chemicals to decompose.
d) Use humour to break the negative spiral – change of point of view influences the system, and again, gives you time.

If the amygdala has already hijacked the brain, it is advisable to take a time-out for 20 minutes and then return again. When dealing further with the conflict, active listening and showing empathy are worth remembering.

An interpretation of a lack of appreciation or offending someone's values may in the interaction in a management team occasionally cause a desire to fight, flee or play dead. These models of behaviour are certainly not the best in an organized change management process. The situation can often be quickly defused by saying: this activates the amygdala, can we express this thing differently?

Elements of success: agility, competence and condition

The obligation of the management is to develop, and a Stellar Team develops itself, too. Development is always about making changes, in which something is changed into something else – which, the developer thinks, is better than before. In order to succeed, the management team needs agility, competence and condition.

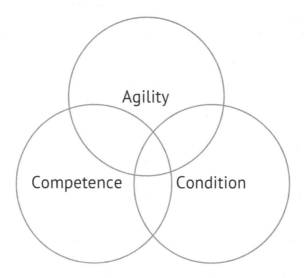

Figure 14.2 Elements for success in change

Agility means flexibility and adaptability in attitude. Often implementation of changes is connected to determined action, actually stubborn pushing. Operations of organizations are, however, linked to so many variables that a successful management team connects the change to flexible structures and phased action plans, which adapt during the iterative process. Agility is often utilization of the characteristics of coaching leadership, being alert and taking action quickly when the time comes. Systemic thinking, and observing wholeness promote agility.

Competence means the ability and know-how to lead the change and to understand the essential models of change. The 8-step model of Kotter is well-known and has been proved in many change processes, although it is often poorly understood. A minimum requirement for competence is that everyone reads the book *Our Iceberg Is Melting* by John Kotter and Holger Rathgeber. It is a compact fable in 160 pages that presents the essentials of Kotter's model.

Condition means mental fitness, energy of performance. In change management it is resilience with its exercised and developed characteristics. The quantity and the quality of changes are constantly increasing, and they offer splendid terrain for daily exercise and raising your condition. Common use of the resilient thinking models of individual team members requires synergic collaboration in the team. (See the next chapter). Then the individual characteristics of resilience become the foundation for top condition of the team.

15 The journey is long when travelling alone

RESOURCE BLINDNESS

Symptoms: Fading faith in resources or delusion of managing well

Resource blindness is in most management team cases blind faith in oneŝ own resources. The first symptom is fairly elevated optimism, so the team often sets goals that are over optimistic and beyond its possibilities. The management does not understand its own resources defect in proportion to the complexity of the objective. *Resource blindness* can also prevent the team from seeing how resources are misallocated and sometimes results in even a realistic goal not being achieved. Without proper treatment the consequences are fatal, for example, a fairly healthy business may be given over to cheap amputation.

A second variation of *resource blindness* is caused by too low optimism. This form is rare in management teams but at an individual level it is classified „almost as a public health problem%in some northern cultures. It blurs faith in oneŝ own resources and causes the secondary symptom of *impaired distance assessment capability*. These patients set their goals too unambitiously with respect to their resources.

Care instructions in Appendix 2: Ŝelf care guide for management teamsÊ

African saying: If you want to go fast, go alone.

If you want to go far, go together.

A thinking management team

The quality of common thinking in the management team influences the journey to the stars. Lazy, instinctive and intuitive thinking is natural for us humans. Instinctive thinking is also connected to predictions, prevailing concepts, authorities, experts and easily available background information. Intellectually, the past gives no guarantee of the future, but the only decisive perspective is the present together with an estimate of the future. We have a tendency to come up with logical explanations for incidents afterwards, even though they were in fact just coincidences. This drift into creating stories may have unpleasant consequences, if it is applied to predicting the future.

Laziness seeks quick explanations, although we should investigate the background more analytically and precisely. Rolf Dobelli from Switzerland describes thinking biases in his book *The Art of Thinking Clearly*. Dobelli runs largely along the same tracks as the Nobel laureate Kahneman when urging criticism and the questioning of „facts‰

> „We often make decisions on instinct and explain our choices afterwards. Many decisions (work, life partner, investment) are made unconsciously. A second later we have built arguments for them. This creates the impression that we made the decision consciously.‰

For instance „the sunk cost fallacy‰hits us when we have invested too much money, time or energy, without any sense. We can find numerous examples of this fallacy in construction and renovation. The initial investment changes into justifying continuing a project, and the more we have wasted money, the greater the pressure to continue will grow.

We are made up of the sum of our decisions. We make plenty of them daily and almost automatically. One‼s entire life is choices. Unfortunately research shows that the more information and complexity, the more we will handle that information automatically and hermeneutically, through our interpretations and assumptions.

A sensing management team

The interaction in a management team takes place on four levels: contact processes, data processes, emotional processes and identity processes. Being aware of these levels enables us to influence these processes. On our Stellar Team journey we will encounter unpleasant things and negative feelings as well, so focus on success has to deal especially with the control of the emotional process.

1. **People live in continuous emotional processes**
    This is a fact that cannot be changed by denial: human beings are emotional beings. We react to changes and unexpected surprises with emotions and dealing with these takes time. In the emotional process we can identify the four main stages of facing up to new things and changes:

    *   contentment with the present state
    *   denial of the need for change, followed by anxiety of denial

- facing the anxiety, handling it and stopping for genuine reflection, which produces peaceful thinking
- accepting the change, at best a gradually growing enthusiasm for new possibilities, and finally energetic implementation.

2. **Treating the emotional process has positive effects**

   Sometimes we need to invest time in treating the emotional process. In practice, this means talking about emotions and feelings in an accepting atmosphere. When the emotions are transmitted by word, even a short conversation helps to advance at a factual level. It also builds trust at the same time.

   Conveying emotions by means of words is conversation, in which we let people express what worries them, annoys, troubles or, on the other hand inspires them right now. Expressing emotions must not lead to grinding things over and over, but at the end you can lead the conversation gently towards strategic themes and other management subjects.

3. **You can develop control of your mind**

   Identifying your own emotions, naming them and accepting them will improve the quality of your thinking. Conscious methods of mind control, e.g. mindfulness exercises, develop your concentration, tolerance to pressure and ability to handle demanding decisions. By using mind control methods we support ourselves and others in handling issues productively, by preventing adverse emotional processes, or self-complacent action.

4. **Emotions are phenomena of organizational system and culture**

   Emotional phenomena are always also community-based. The transmission of emotions is a feature of herd animals. We can use emotions of our own, our team and subordinates as indicators of the progress of operations. Emotions are also transferred in organizations, from one team to another. Analysing these phenomena develops emotional intelligence and helps a deeper understanding of the situation in the organization.

EXPLORE THIS: WHAT IS BEHIND THE EMOTION?

Is there some less pleasant emotion prevailing in our team right now? Let us assume that there is an interpretation behind that emotion, and behind the interpretation there is an incident or a phenomenon. So, which incidents and phenomena do we need to deal with when we feel these emotions?

A coaching management team

A Stellar Team will fly steadily and efficiently towards the Guiding Star, when it is being coached towards insights and stretching itself. In a traditional culture the discussion features yesterdayŝ problems and culprits. In a coaching culture we reflect on the here and now, focusing on goals and solutions, which will bring success tomorrow. As the business environment becomes more complex, it is the coaching approach which adds agility that will function best.

> WAKE UP! COACHING MEANS A SIMPLE WAY OF ACTING, IN WHICH YOU DON'T GIVE ANY ADVICE BUT . . .
> . . . YOU CHALLENGE OTHERS WITH YOUR QUESTIONS TO CREATE SOLUTIONS OF THEIR OWN.

In successful organizations the management team has to channel this involving and inspiring model to the entire organization.

1. **Coaching leaders accept others to coach them**
    A Stellar Team implements mutual coaching and mutual sharing of problems in its own work. This means being exposed to coaching by every member. Additionally this will build common understanding and strengthen trust.
2. **Coaching leaders coach others instead of advising**
    In a Stellar Team we find lots of questions and positive questioning. That creates space for thinking. A coaching working style suits equally dealing with personal growth issues and business challenges.
3. **Coaching leaders spread a coaching culture in the organization**
    A Stellar Team cascades a coaching culture consciously into the entire organization. This means conveying a positive mind-set for possibilities to succeed. It is faith in human development. Through coaching leadership the Stellar Team creates inspiration to achieve dazzling goals, which requires the management team to really stretch itself.
4. **Coaching leaders put effort into success focused action and rely on people's autonomy**
    A Stellar Team directs energy into finding solutions and supporting the autonomy of people. Coaching leaders do not stick to problems and failures. There are two key issues: how could things be at best and which small actions will make us progress daily in that direction?

TRY THIS: Success focused coaching for 10 minutes

When someone approaches you with a problem, ask him or her if you can help to reflect on that problem for 10 minutes. Select questions from the list below and use the given time for each group of questions.

1. Success focused questions about the goal, 7 minutes

    *   How should it be when it is solved?
    *   How will it work when it works?
    *   What does it look like when it is solved?

- How would you describe the solution?
- What is happening then?
- What features can you see in it?
- What is the most important aspect of it?
- What benefits does it offer?
- To whom? To whom else?
- How does it affect you?
- What is the goal in this?
- What important thing(s) does it enable?
- What else?
- How does it influence other functions?
- What is the meaning of this total solution for you?
- For your organization?
- What is the most important goal in this?

2. Questions clarifying present resources, 2 minutes

- What do you/your team/we already have for this goal?
- How much is already planned?
- Which steps have you taken?
- Linked to this, what have you done before?
- What resources do you have?
- Which competences and know-how?
- What are you/your team/we good at?

3. Action oriented questions for the future, 1 minute

- What will be the first step that takes you/us towards the goal?
- Who does what and when – and how will it be concluded when the step has been taken?
- What are the following steps?
- Action plan . . .?

Reflect by yourself at the end on what you observed in the other person and on what you learned – all in 10 minutes.

Coaching leadership as philosophy and modus operandi

Developing into a Stellar Team succeeds when the individualŝ action and behaviour changes to the right direction. Principles of personality psychology, however, confirm that permanent behavioural change will become a reality only if thinking changes. Ultimately, the way to a Stellar Team is the development of common thinking. In everyday life there are always opportunities to practice the desired behaviours. There is nothing to prevent common success, when we are tuned to the same frequency on thinking and mind-set levels.

The coaching leadership approach gathers together the wisdom of the development of management teams. In their book on coaching leadership, Marjo-Riitta Ristikangas and Vesa Ristikangas (2010) have entered into the core of coaching leadership. They crystallize the concept in a few points of view, which when interpreted into the language of management teams provides an opportunity to customize the way of thinking and acting together.

> *„Coaching leadership is a holistic way of being, influencing others and being influenced. It is appreciative, inclusive and goal-oriented collaboration, in which the potential of an individual is released for use in the team and organization. The team potential, in turn, supports the empowerment of individuals. Coaching leadership is based on trust, and this belongs to everyone‰*

Influential process of a team

> *Coaching leadership is a holistic way of being, influencing others and being influenced.*

Coaching leadership is a mutual team competence that should be holistic and at hand for all. The attention is 100% on joint action, not on mobiles or laptops. In addition, equality is the foundation of the coaching approach. When management team members discuss and influence each other, the issues are not agreed in advance, but individuals are interested in and influenced by the thoughts of each other. At the same time, they have an opportunity to influence others while expressing their thoughts out loud. Attitudes to each other are healthy, not arrogant nor degrading.

The way of thinking and acting, which unleashes the potential

> *It is appreciative, inclusive and goal-oriented collaboration, in which the potential of an individual is released for use in the team and organization. The team potential, in turn, supports the empowerment of individuals.*

Coaching leadership is crystallized in three keywords that form the foundation of a Stellar Team.

(a)   When the attitude is **appreciative**, no one needs to seek protection. Then it is safe to make mistakes and take risks, as you know the others are on the same side. Everyone can be himself or herself, with their different strengths and weaknesses.

(b)   Coaching leadership is **involving** collaboration. When the team has created a culture of collaboration, its competences come into wide common use. By *involving* we mean asking questions and activating others – through different forms of collaboration both in meetings and between them.

(c) The third key element of leadership coaching is **goal orientation** and its use in daily work. Many management teams are very much goal oriented, which is good. This characteristic on its own however is imperfect and therefore its real power remains untapped. When goal orientation is connected to an appreciative and involving approach, the road is wide open to the stars.

Coaching leadership is based on trust, and this belongs to everyone

Lastly, there we have two reminders that are at the core of the coaching management team. First, no team can grow without mutual trust. Mutual trust is the foundation for joint development. Second, an important perspective is that coaching leadership belongs to all. It is not the sole right of the management team leader. When all management team members start to relate to each other in an appreciative and involving way, with a common goal in their minds, nothing will be able to prevent the team from triumphing!

How to create synergy?

Good collaboration is based on cohesion and on team synergy. In other words, the team members have to experience attractive fellowship inside the team and have to create an accumulative combined effect out of their personal qualities. In practice the management team has to strive towards cooperation and splendid results.

The starting point for synergy in business is always that the organization must generate better results in collaboration than by the sum of its members acting separately. The number and quality of positive factors affect team cohesion. When cohesion increases, the synergy of the team increases, and vice versa. How do we create such an excellent snowball effect?

Synergy is an emergent phenomenon, which is born and shaped in complex systems. Emergent means that the pieces click together by themselves, and create a combined effect of accumulative factors, if appropriate factors are present. An example of a complex system is a management team, which consists of individuals with different qualities – strengths and even weaknesses. To put it clearly:

> *A synergistic team combines the strength of its members and, at the same time, eliminates negative effects of single weaknesses in individual members.*

This is the way a team will attain the results it is pursuing.

We take here as an example one of the characteristics of resilience – optimism – and two different management teams that need to make an investment decision.

> 1. *A management team without synergy*
>   *A person calling himself an ultra realist, i.e. the least optimistic member of the team, announces instantly, that the money will be wasted. Thus, even the most optimistic in the team gives up and says: I'm not going to venture my comments, let it be.*
>
> 2. *A synergistic management team*
>   *The strongest optimist in the team declares immediately that this project will succeed and the team will at least learn a lot, which will justify that investment. The least optimistic member of the team answers: Personally, I don't believe that, but in this team, I am prepared to give my full support!*

In celebratory speeches it is often said: in our organization 1+1 makes more than 2! Why do all teams not exceed this mathematical result that is so often talked up? Which factors do they actually miss, if the accumulative effect, i.e. synergy, does not emerge within the team? These factors are powerful and familiar and they have also been presented earlier in this book:

(1) Our management team lacks common goals, or at least, they are unclear.
(2) Our management team is, in reality, a pack of lone wolves running around.
(3) I have no influence in the management team; I am not listened to and not taken into account.
(4) The participation of other members is a sham; our management team has free riders.
(5) The interaction among the members of our management team is very weak; no questions, no listening, no conversation – and silence when it comes to obvious issues.
(6) I do not feel that I am valued – in fact, no one does.
(7) The management team members play solo outside the team, they do not hold to joint decisions.
(8) Our management team does not make decisions, or at least the implementation of decisions is lame; we do not achieve what is agreed.

If a management team member feels that even one of the above is true, that person will no longer give his/her full contribution to the team. He or she does not bring a „full 1% to the summation and unless someone is going to compensate for this shortfall, the result will definitely be less than the sum of its parts.

What is the wonder glue that helps us to assemble a complete puzzle of incomplete pieces – or even to assemble a management team that is greater than the sum of its parts? That requires determined building of synergy. Synergy is the creation and strengthening of the cumulative effect. The prerequisite for synergy is a shared motivation and a dependence on common success. Synergy strengthens collaboration, when we take care of the structures that steer members to participate, influence and implement decisions.

How can we knock this eight-item list into shape in practice? The simplest way is to ask the management team, blow by blow, how these things should be. For example, how should things be concerning the clarity of the common goals? A good discussion will ensue, which is a clear step towards synergy.

CHECK THIS: Once more

Even if the goals already are common and clear, they are still worth checking one more time. Ask the team members to individually prepare a one-minute presentation on your common goals. Synergy will strengthen, even if everyone presents the same thing, word for word. Equally synergy will also be supported, if there are differences in the presentations.

How does synergistic collaboration produce more than the sum of its parts?

Creating synergy is affected crucially by the relationships within the team. The following three key factors are essential for results:

1. **Motivation of collaboration**, which is promoted by

    - attractive common goals
    - identified mutual dependency

2. **Structures** that enable synergy and make participating rewarding, i.e.

    - enabling participation
    - enabling influencing
    - enabling decision making

3. **Diversity**, because in practice, the sum of different members of the team can be more than the sum of its parts, i.e.

    - selecting team members aims at diversity
    - team members are supported to acquire competences that differ

---

CHALLENGE: Synergy or not?

Explore the following eight items and explain how they have been fulfilled in practice in your management team. How could you develop each item?

---

1. We secure common goals – Are we united behind our goals, are they clear to all of us in practice, too, and jointly inspiring?
2. We create mutual dependence – Does common success require all of us to do his or her own work, does everyonês work have an influence on someone elsês work?
3. We strengthen everyonês influence on the team – Does each of us influence this team, is everyone important, is everyone heard in the team?
4. We demand of everyone 100% participation – Is each of us fully involved, putting himself/herself on the line, committed and keeping promises?
5. We implement good interaction – Do we ask questions, listen and discuss, are we present together?
6. We show appreciative understanding to each other – Do we show appreciation, can we disagree, do we accept each other as different human beings?
7. We are a united team – Do we have a uniform message, are we visibly acting as an integrated team?
8. We make decisions and take care of implementation – Do we implement our decisions, do we take care of follow-up and completion of decisions?

Effective means of building synergy

1. Involvement

Management teams often work with a star model, in which the leader is the centre and team members are the points of the star. In this model, interaction takes place only between the centre and the points. In other words, team members report to the team leader. This kind of team is far from a real team, and we can only wonder how this serves – or worships – the leader. It is also easy to guess, how much this frustrates management team members while wasting their time and misusing resources.

To change this situation four really difficult things are required:

*   Material on the matters to be decided at the meeting needs to be submitted to all in good time before the meeting
*   Everyone must prepare himself/herself for the meeting
*   The management team leader must create the possibility for interaction
*   Everyone must participate in the handling of matters.

Many of us have certainly experienced so called „involvement‰ The first two of the previous points may succeed, but unfortunately the latter two tend to go like this in many management teams:

> *Leader:*   *Any comment on the previous proposal? – Anybody? – Shall we*
>   *approve it? – Charlie?*
> *Charlie:*   *Sorry, could you repeat that?*
> *Leader:*   *Any comment?*
> *Charlie:*   *Just ok. (– Someone else may hum approvingly)*

How does a real Stellar Team act? The Stellar Team differs from the previous significantly, because it has its own rules:

* silence is a sign of absence, not assent
* if there is nothing to improve in the proposal of the colleague, then it must at least be praised
* even if there is something to improve in the proposal of the colleague, it still must be praised.

At the beginning, developing a Stellar Team may require the leader to firmly challenge the team. Everyone in the team is requested to comment, even by finger pointing to each member in turn. The question „What was good in the proposal?‰ requires a commentary. The team should first note all the positive aspects of the proposal and only then make corrective suggestions. This surely takes more time than a sigh or a hum, but it also forms a totally new setting for all matters under consideration. Such a setting creates synergy, which will harness all brain-power to the benefit of common issues.

2. Appreciation

How do you know that you are appreciated? Do you know it for sure? Think about a person that you appreciate. Does he or she really know about your appreciation? Appreciation or the lack of it is regrettably often based on guesswork.

> *A supervisor described movingly what it takes to be appreciated:*
>
> „*My boss has* **told** *me that he appreciates my initiative, and he* **shows** *me opportunities where I can actually make use of that initiative‰*

Every team could develop their collaboration enormously by telling each other clearly, what they appreciate, what makes them glad, inspired, happy . . .

3. Integrating interaction

A synergistic management team needs situations in which it can systematically implement a „building block dialogue‰together. A solution focused trainer colleague, Harri Hirvihuhta, has illustrated this with a playground metaphor, which describes the dialogue of two children playing.

Destroying interaction:
– This could be a house here – No, not there, but here – But itŝ gonna be a terraced house – No, a block of flats – Then I will break it down – Then I will tell my daddy – Then my daddy will punch your daddy . . . etc.

Integrating interaction, or a snowballing dialogue:
– Yes, and then this here will make a garage – Yeah, and here we can build a fence – Yes, and the all the cars would come here – Yeah, and here will be a street . . . etc.

It is very worthwhile to test the „yes, and%dialogue model of the latter example.

4. Implementation

Many of us have a need for completion, which is a strong legacy from the days of the caveman. If I did not get my shelter ready before dark, I was exposed to predators. Seeing a completed project produces satisfaction for a reason. Usually, as a result of management team meetings we are unable to even see a primitive shelter made out of twigs! A synergistic management team implements decisions and seeks the joy of completion consciously by listing at the beginning of meetings decisions from previous meetings, which have been implemented and taken to completion.

Three basic needs of a traveller

Everybody undoubtedly knows Maslowŝ hierarchy of needs: physiological – safety – belongingness and love – esteem – self-actualization. David McClellandŝ achievement motivation theory says that the lower level basic needs are congenital, so he started exploring with his team the higher needs, which are learned. It is probably easy to recognize management colleagues from the following.

1. Need for achievement

Do you have in your management team members who have a strong need to become successful and to strive forward in their lives? These people

• strive for personal success rather than for reward from it
• want to do things better than before, they seek for a task, where they can be personally responsible for their performance and for producing solutions

- want to have feedback quickly, in order to see the direction of their development
- are not gamblers, they only take assignments that are not too easy, nor too demanding, and they want to take responsibility for everything themselves, so nothing is left to chance.

2. *Need for affiliation*

Do you have in your management team members who have a strong need for human relationships and a desire to be with people? These people

- want to be liked and accepted by others
- prefer to seek assignments where you collaborate instead of competing
- favour organizations in which decisions are made unanimously

3. *Need for power*

Do you have in your management team members who have a strong need to influence other people and make them do things that they would normally not do? They

- want to be „in charge‰
- want to influence people, control others and be powerful
- seek competitive and position based assignments, and put more effort into increasing their prestige than into performance efficiency.

How are the above needs linked to good collaboration? The members of a Stellar Team have all three basic needs in balance. The team members also identify the needs of each other in different situations and are able to take these into consideration. As the described needs are learned, we can also develop them through conscious action in our neuroplastic brains. Do you lack some of these needs in your management team? How do you observe that lack in practice?

Figure PS.IV Goals

Core of Part IV: Roles, resilience and synergy on our journey to the stars

In this book we are undertaking a metaphoric journey to the stars, which means we are developing the management team into a Stellar Team that raises its operations to a new level of results. The stars are far away but our guiding star shows us the direction. In spite of space orientation we are still on the ground and firmly on this planet. In Part IV we have explored in particular the means of developing the management team. Essential insights and questions on the journey to the stars are the following:

- Members of the Stellar Team are aware of their different roles. How do we ensure that we know how to take on these roles?
- The Stellar Team̂s thinking and actions are high class. How do we implement coaching leadership in a success focused way?
- The Stellar Team deals even with unexpected changes. How do we develop the sense of control and the characteristics of our resilience, how do we overcome together the amygdala hijack attempts?
- The Stellar Team collaborates efficiently, it interacts and develops constantly. How do we build true synergy? How do we develop our collaboration further?

The journey of the Stellar
Management Team continues . . .

STELLAR
MANAGEMENT
TEAM

The Stellar Team has arrived at a galactic service area. The journey towards the guiding star has inspired the team to strive for better performance and reminded it of the importance of collaboration and of the comprehensive approach to its common management mission. Stellar Team members have to summarize now the key doctrines and ideas of their development journey. The Stellar Team wants to remind itself, and all teams that are departing on a journey, of the power of cooperation. Finally, we present the most important star tips that will inspire our Stellar Team to a new flight, towards a new guiding star.

1. We are curious

We consciously explore our action, we snoop around the shady areas of our thinking, we scan for weak signals around us. We do not settle just for hearing and reading, but also go on to experience real-world events. While experiencing, we understand how our customers react and how our products and services are received by them.

2. We learn by questioning

We are prepared to doubt our own thinking. We seek for deep understanding and multidimensional thinking. We are aware that the ability to learn fast is a competitive advantage. We reserve systematically time for learning new things. Each of us is aware of his or her personal learning style.

3. We reflect systematically

We reflect both on common and personal action, because this is the most essential method of learning. We do it continuously and always when an opportunity arises. We wonder about things from different perspectives.

4.　We trust each other

We trust each other. Each of us can tell openly, even personally unfavourable things to the team. We are open; we do not hide information, because in this way our business decisions are on a realistic basis. We consciously act openly in order to solve issues, not to point the finger.

5.　We enrich our interaction

We do not compete with each other but rather we create together an enriching interaction. We are constructive. We want to know, understand and accept the different backgrounds and operating styles of the others. We create a positive spirit in our team by lifting up each other. We remember to laugh often, because our demanding work also demands joy and lightness.

6.　We appreciate our colleagues

We talk of each other with appreciation and in a positive light outside the team. We are absolutely aware that a mutual loyalty and constructive culture are being generated by the stories that we tell about each other and our team.

7.　We argue constructively

We know how to discuss even emotional and problematic issues together, openly, and so thoroughly, that a consensus emerges. We see different and conflicting opinions as an asset, not as a threat.

In our discussion we are also prepared to investigate the accuracy of our own thinking. A part of our discussion is constant reflection on our own action and thinking. By reflection we can clarify our experiences, construct new information and find new perspectives.

8.　We show our humanity

We face each other both in the roles of leaders and human beings. We know that everyone has their good and bad moments, good and bad sides. In our management and team companionship we want to be with others as whole human beings and not just as goal managers.

9.　We always play for the team

We are as individuals competent and capable of doing efficient individual work, but in the management team our principal goal is to work together. We mould the management team̂s views and operational decisions out of joint information collection and by means of common reflection. We act consistently and in alignment outside the meetings. We speak in the „we-form‰ and display solidarity.

10. We coach each other

We coach each other and share the problems of our work, which means allowing the others to coach us. We offer to each other as individuals and as a team a coaching approach as solution philosophy, whether it be to do with personal growth or business challenges. This is asking questions, positive questioning and, above all, creating space for the other person's own thinking.

11. We believe in the potential of individuals and teams

We show our positive mind-set towards the possibilities for success. We communicate our faith in human development and create through coaching leadership an inspiration to be able to implement enormous goals, which in turn demands that we too have to stretch ourselves. We spread the coaching culture intentionally in our entire organization.

12. We do everything for our customers

We are committed to developing our organization and operations in order to produce an excellent customer experience as regards the quality of our products and services. We are interested in improvement ideas from amongst our employees and we put systematic effort into laying the roots of customer centred thinking into our organization.

A development journey is like space: it is endless. Developing a management team into a Stellar Team is the continuous development of thinking together. This in turn is followed by the development of seeing and acting together. Collaboration is the factor that makes the difference between a Stellar Management Team and an ordinary management team. The Stellar Management Team is in every way on an entirely different results level.

> „*They used to say that if Man was meant to fly, he'd have wings.*
> *But he did fly. He discovered he had to‰*
> – Captain Kirk, TV series *Star Trek: Return*
> *to Tomorrow* (1968)

THE END

Appendix 1
Coaching guide for management teams

In the world of sports every individual athlete and every team has their own coach. Especially in team sports, the significance of a coach is more emphasized. There is certainly not a single world-class team, aiming at international events on their own – without a coach. If good sports results demand a coach, why not a management team aiming to be a Stellar Team?

Coaching – individual co-driver on your journey to the stars

Coaching has become a permanent development method in organizations over the past two decades. The number of professional coaches is constantly growing. Coaching is widely known in the field of Human Resources administration, but among supervisors some incorrect thinking still prevails. Here are some corrections:

- *Coaching is not a method for problematic cases. You do not send an awkward person to coaching to be „healed‰ or „changed‰*
  BUT coaching is a development method, in which the essential factor is the coachee̕s own free will to develop him or herself. No one can be coached by force.
- *A coach does not tell what the coachee should do in order to reach the goal.*
  BUT the coach is a companion for thinking and his or her duty is to support the clients in their own thinking. This requires good interaction skills. A coach leads the coachee to think and challenges the client to develop himself or herself by means of good questions.
- *A coach does not have to be an experienced manager to be able to coach managers and leaders.*
  BUT a top coach is recognized by his or her skill of being able to adapt the core competences of coaching. The coach is a professional of individual development, not an expert on a single substance area.
- *A coach does not define in advance the themes and methods for handling them.*
  BUT the coach̕s duty is to follow the agenda of the coachee only. The coach is at the service of the coachee!

All these previously described aspects create an impression of the world of individual coaching, where a professional coach and coachee build their confidential relationship in order to serve the goals of the coachee. The International Coaching Federation (ICF) is the association for professional coaches, and ICF defines individual coaching concisely as

> *partnering with clients in a thought-provoking and creative process that inspires them to maximize their personal and professional potential.*

Thus, in individual coaching the focus is on the benefit derived out of the unused potential of the coachee. A coach for the highest management is often an external professional coach, and often solely speaking of issues using their right names may help. Insights and new perspectives are born, when you have an opportunity to handle the issues and take them out of your mind by saying them out loud. Professor David Clutterbuck, who is a pioneer in the world of coaching, confirms the same. He states that coaching is primarily the development of thinking. When thinking becomes clearer and changed, even the actions taken will change.

Why does coaching work? Research shows that its efficacy relies on the fact that the coaching is used to influence the coachee's power to make his or her own decisions, the so-called Volition (Parppei 2008). The coachee says out loud what he or she is going to do over the next few weeks in order to achieve the goals established, and the mere reporting obligation initiates the necessary impetus. Words become actions and the change becomes a reality. Coaching has an effect.

The effectiveness of coaching has also been stated in many studies, in which the return on investment of coaching (ROI) has been measured. The effectiveness has been measured also on the level of confidence, human resources development, or change of behaviour, which all affect the profitability of business and finally the return on investment. Coaching seems to be a quite profitable investment, showing even at a minimum level ROI higher 20% (Lisa Ann Edwards, head of Talent Management at Corbis and founder of Bloom Coaching Institute). Individual coaching has an effect, which is positively visible also in profitability.

A management team on its journey to the stars needs individual solutions in order to get the best out of the engines of team members. It is wise to develop individual solutions to release the potential of every director or manager, and to support the desire of development towards common goals.

A Stellar Team knows, however, that which Wageman et al. (2008) have stated in their research:

> The capacity of a team will hardly improve, even if each of its members has personal coaching to develop their own leadership qualities.

Developing a team is an area of expertise, totally of its own. A team reaching out for stars needs team coaching, if together they want to achieve top performance.

Team coaching – boost your engine on the way to the stars

> *The understanding of team coaching is at this moment at the same level as the understanding of personal coaching 20 years ago!*
>
> (Hawkins 2011)

Professor Peter HawkinsÊstatement tells us something about the life cycle of coaching. Alongside individual coaching practices a team and community centred way of thinking and acting is growing. In particular, concerning management teams, team coaching and its practices need clarifying. What is team coaching of management teams about? What is the difference between team coaching and other development methods like facilitation, consulting or team training?

Clarity for definitions

There are a few principal thought leaders, who have started working on the clarification of team coaching at the management team level.

> Team coaching is action that aims to improve the efficiency of the team, and it takes place in influencing the internal interaction of team members (Wageman et al. 2008).
>
> Team coaching is coaching the team to achieve a common goal, and the focus is both on individual performance and team practices and performance (Thornton 2010).
>
> Team coaching is about the improvement of team performance and its processes, which is implemented through reflection and dialogue (Clutterbuck 2009).

All the previous definitions focus in their management team adaptation on how to create ideal conditions in a team. In addition to internal functionality, a holistic team coaching also takes into account the system that shows collective leadership in and around the management team. Then team coaching becomes systemic team coaching, which includes management team development widely.

> Systemic team coaching is a process in which the team coach works together with the team, when it is assembled, and also when it is separated. Team coaching focuses on improving the collective performance and practices of collaboration, as well as on developing collective leadership, in order to promote more efficient influence of essential stakeholders.
>
> (Hawkins 2011)

The previous definitions express the core of team coaching. Based on our own experience and inspired by the thinkers named, we explore further some different perspectives on holistic team coaching at management team level.

The management team of a technical wholesaler was quite large with its 11 members. More than half had been more than 10 years in the management team. William, the new CEO, started a few years ago and noticed very soon the difficulties in the operation of the team. He started a renewal and succeeded in recruiting new competences, and above all, in bringing fresh thinking to the team. The monthly meetings of the team during the last 6 months, however, had been anything but energizing. At almost every meeting, the members had started picking on each other, which led to open emotional outbursts. William was in a tight spot on several occasions and felt helpless in keeping the players in the „playground‰ under control. Finally, William acquired backing for himself, in the form of a pair of team coaches who worked as co-coaches. Their first activity was to observe the team. The following phenomena were noticed during a full day meeting.

Mutual rivalry

This organization is the sales company of a global corporation. The local management team consists of several sales unit directors, most of whom have worked independently for many years. The reward system has supported individual activity, in which the ownership of the customer has been emphasized. The new CEO and his talk of cooperation are akin to disturbing an anthill. At worst, the companyŝ salespeople now compete with each other for customers – after all, your own incentives are the most important.

As regards the operations of the Management Team this rivalry manifests itself such that each sales unit director defends his/her own territories and notes the excellent processes they have developed. Over the years, everyone has modified their practices on how to lead their units. The CEOŝ beautiful collaboration rhetoric has been drowned out by the noise of competition.

Sales vs. support function

Sales people are the royals in the organization and their actions are not to be criticized. On the contrary they have every right to evaluate and blame others. During the past months hallway discussions have concluded that the most crucial obstacle for sales is the support function. There is neither understanding nor action as regards the wishes of the sales people. In addition, support functions do not realize how customers think and what is best for them. The sales director openly brings this message to the management team, communicating at the same time that the sales department has no problem.

The setting is complete. Thereŝ a battle in which the support function defends itself against attacks and the sales ‚locomotives‛ try to hold on to their story until the end. The CEO looks on and tries to stop the gainsaying. The battle ends when the CEO manages to move the focus onto a new topic. However, the tension remains and energy is wasted, unfortunately.

Skipping issues and monologues

Management team meetings are often long in duration, and no wonder. Debates are emotional, justifying the accuracy of one͗s own views. Words are used efficiently and artfully, and masses of interpretations are created between the lines. Disputes go on about people in general, their thoughts and attitudes, without names. There is always someone in the team, who will react. The more difficult issue, the more likely attention will be directed totally elsewhere. Skipping issues effectively ensures that the real issues are guaranteed not to be dealt with.

Emphasizing "personal"

A certain sentence is repeated often: „Don͗ take this personally‰ It is repeated like a mantra, even though continuous „taking personally‰ forms a chain in the discussion. However, it creates a momentary impression that the individual has been understood. Discussion in the management team forms a chain of defence speeches, which do not promote dealing with the issues at hand nor moving towards any conclusion.

Strong voices

There are strong individuals in the management team and their voices are sometimes loud. Truths about the team situation are thrown out in the middle of the meeting. Although no one responds to them, they form an interesting basis for team dialogue.

Person X: „I think everybody ought to do the same as I have done. During the past 2 years I have cleared all the fat out of my team. I have set tough goals and made my team members commit to them. I have made my conclusions about those for whom it hasn͗ worked out, and I have let them go. This can be seen in my efficiency figures. I am pleased to consult your units, in case you need help‰

Person Y: „We have a problem, which is in our culture. The working climate has never been as poor as it is now. But nevertheless, the climate here in the management team doesn͗ look any better‰

Both voices are cleverly ignored in the management team. If the issue becomes too personal and starts to hot up, attention must be directed elsewhere. The entire team sighs with relief and the solitary whistle-blower is excluded to lick his or her wounds.

Lack of leadership is apparent and tangible

William has worked a lot as CEO to make space for his way of thinking. The previous CEO controlled the system sovereignly and used his power ruthlessly; a solid climate of fear became rooted in the management culture. In everyday life, it was seen in primitive ways of coping: escaping, dodging and hedging. For a few years, William tried to build a new culture without fear. Some results could already be seen – after all, he had received a lot of positive feedback from his subordinates concerning the dramatic change in climate for the better.

The shadow of the change became visible very quickly in the management team. In the past William had kept the troops in line with fear, but now power had been transferred to some management team members. Their refined verbal sorties below the belt and tendency to victimize often caused unpleasant situations, in which William's good intentions were toothless. His wishes and talks of the importance of collaboration were no longer effective. Fear was no longer recognizable, but the need for protection was still, however, constant.

Goals and results of team coaching in management teams

1. **Focusing on the team as a whole**, in which the team coach supports the team and its functionality with a selection of methods. The team is an entity of its own, ant it is more important than any of its members.
2. **Clarifying the purpose of existence (mission) and the guiding star (vision) of the management team**. It is important for the management team to define the mission and vision of its own, which are aligned to the mission and the vision of the organization.
3. **Strengthening the collective leadership in the management team** and responsibility to steer towards the common goal. On their way to the stars members put effort primarily into joint benefit, not focusing on their own interests.
4. **Building bridges of collaboration** between members of the management team, and securing collaboration also outside the meetings. The meetings are like warm-ups as the real game takes place between the meetings.
5. **Enhancing cooperation in the meetings of the management team** aiming at wise decisions and shared commitment.
6. **Directing the attention of the management team to essential stakeholders** and to taking them into account in developing the business.
7. **Creating prerequisites in the management team to widely influence business operations**. On the way to the stars, responding merely to surrounding changes is not sufficient, rather active influence on the entire business environment is required.

At the core of team coaching operates the entire team, which is served by the wide range of expertise of the team coach. The results become visible when a professional team coach begins to see the teamîs activities as part of a broader organizational entity, and he or she is able to take advantage of that as a part of the coaching process. The team coach becomes an enabler who creates conditions to utilize the potential of the team throughout the organizational system. Then attention is no longer just on team interaction dynamics, but also on essential themes of everyday work, such as dynamics of decision-making, strategic choices and their implementation, and on relationship management of key customers. A team coach directs the management team discussion to the essentials – on the way to the stars.

Team coach supports towards the guiding star

In individual coaching the coach walks along with the coachee and opens up opportunities for insights and development of personal thinking. Individual coaching takes place either face to face or virtually – anyway as a bilateral learning process. The coach asks questions, challenges thinking and actions taken towards the goal.

How does individual coaching differ from team coaching? A lot, really a lot. The fundamentals, of course, remain, but ways of doing things differ significantly. A team coach working with management teams lands up in the middle of the intricacies of group dynamics and the rationality of business making. The team coach has a holistic perspective on the management team, and he or she is able to adapt the action to the situation of the management team and to operational necessities. A professional team coach can be identified by the following practices:

- **Team coaches draw the foundation for their action from the philosophy of coaching**. Good questions, the ability to listen and the skill of being together with a group are the foundation for building collaboration.
- **Team coaches adapt their activities to the situation and needs of the team, serving the benefit of the team**. Team coaches may have pre-planned action in their minds. Skilful team coaches are able to spontaneously use tools from their toolboxes, for the benefit of the team.
- **Team coaches see and make visible phenomena that are essential for the development of the team**. Team coaches think out loud and name phenomena that they observe in the team. They are experts on group dynamics and they note their observations for the benefit of the team.
- **Team coaches challenge to develop**. Team coaching of management teams is efficient when the coach has the courage to steer the team outside its comfort zone. Bringing up issues that are essential to individuals and to the team promotes development in team dynamics.
- **Team coaches are co-travellers and awakeners**, who have sufficient understanding of the logic in the business and in the dynamics of business processes. In addition to their role as a coach, they also need facilitation and consulting skills.

TRY THIS: We as a team

Take a moment for these questions in your management team and be amazed by the results that crystallize in some 20 minutes.

1. State your as-is-state on a scale of 1–10; how do we act now as a team? Everyone gives an individual evaluation and then you calculate the average.
2. State your to-be-state on a scale of 1–10; how do we have to act as a team, in order to achieve our goals? (If this does not require any development from you, then try to exceed or double your goal.) Everyone gives an individual evaluation and then you calculate the average.
3. Describe what new things you can observe in your team action once you have achieved your goal? Discuss how the action as a good team has become visible. How does it look, sound and feel?
4. What are the two factors in our behaviour or ways to operate that we will change in order to narrow the difference between the as-is and to-be state? Discuss the alternatives that might be useful for you as a team. Choose together two behaviours or ways of operation, and then commit all together to changing them.
5. We presume that team members can personally influence the difference between as-is and to-be state by changing two important things in theirs behaviours or ways of operation. Choose individually two behaviours or ways of operation that everyone will personally change in order to narrow the difference between the as-is and to-be state. Agree on how each team member will report monthly on personal development to the team.

Appendix 2
Self care guide for management teams

Diagnoses and care instructions:

JDI syndrome, AJDS
Novophobia
Management team swell
Management team vertigo
Image delusion
Secret society paralysis
Meeting syndrome
Goal itch, malignant leadership, human blindness
Culture abscess
Sacred cow disease
Power scabies
Diversity indigestion, condensation of collective irrationality
Silo inflammation
Positivity intolerance, yummy-yummy allergy, fault eye
Management team oedema
Boss constipation
Change motion sickness
Resource blindness and advice deafness

JDI syndrome, AJDS

Forming common will is paralyzed in the team and co-operation is an illusion

JDI syndrome (JDI = Just-Do-It) begins to show due to everyday working pressure of management team members. The disease spreads in the team by means of impatient temperament and performance euphoria addiction of individual members. The entire management team will change to JDI-positive and start to work being seemingly over-energized – a state, which is achieved by a quick allocation of tasks, so that each task is always dedicated to only one team member.

Sometimes JDI develops into hazardous *AJDS* (Acquired Judgement Deficiency Syndrome). Then cooperation between the management team members and joint reflection disappear completely, and the team becomes a compulsory rubber stamp for individual proposals made by its members. In fortunate cases the speedy AJDS team may confirm a lot of good decisions, and even produce the illusion of management team collaboration. Sadly, many well-known examples show that fortune and illusion-based cooperation always lead to arrogance and on to inevitable destruction.

JDI and *AJDS* are apparently incurable, but compliance with the collaboration principles of the book *Stellar Management Teams* (Ristikangas, Rinne) will eliminate all the harmful symptoms and the management team will be even capable of reaching the stars.

Novophobia

Paralysis in unprecedented, first-time experiences

Novophobia is a dangerous state of fear, if it appears in a management team. It is a caveman type of fear of new and strange things, and it „compels%you to make safe choices. It suggests that it is best to do so as you have always been doing, or in very bold cases, to do the same as your competitor does. There is a belief that experiments always have costs, so it is better to stay on the beaten path and think the same way as before. *Novophobia* helped humans in unhurried prehistoric times to stay alive, but in a modern changing world it causes denial of renewal and leads to the path of destruction.

Novophobia care

In *novophobia* the key issue is security. The recommended treatments of *novophobia* are all drugs that expand thinking safely, so drugs and chemicals are out of the question. Good questions are effective when submitted in a safe atmosphere – that is, without pressure for change, unconditional choice or the necessity of making a decision – as well as an appreciative and investigative approach to phenomena occurring in the system.

Management team swell

Action becomes blurred and decision-making will be even paralyzed

Management team swell is caused by too shallow thinking. Most management teams claim they want to focus more on the strategic than the operational. This is looking far ahead and planning how you will get there. It is a noble task – it requires great wisdom and not just anyone cannot do it. If the management team doesnî care for strategy, then who? Supposedly not the board of directors?

In practice, the management teams have often a similar complaint: we have a meeting every week but the reserved three hours are never enough as there are so many operational matters! They are important tasks that require wisdom and determination. And not just anyone can do these either! If the management team does not take care of these operational matters, who will? Supposedly not the employees?

Management team swell begins to show symptoms when the management team wants to decide on operational matters. Unfortunately, there are indefinite numbers of them for every week.

Care of management team swell

To avoid *management team swell* the management team has to focus on strategy. In practice, it has to climb up to an observation tower for its meetings. Then the operative issues will remain down on the ground and they will only look far distant from the top of the tower. From there you can see how the organization is advancing towards the strategic goals. This advance does not need to be observed from the viewing tower several times a month. In this way each member has time for coaching leadership with their own team members, which is in fact the operational management of the strategy.

Management team swell can be prevented when shallow thinking is tackled with two core questions:

1. Do we have to take action on this issue now or will something bad happen/ something good not happen, if we donî take action? – If taking action seems to be necessary, then:
2. To whom do we delegate the action, or do we really have to do it ourselves, and will the action not be done, if we do not act?

The duty of the highest management team is to secure that the organization has a clear strategy, which enables operative decision-making on other levels. Important people in the observation tower must not suffer from *management team swell*.

Management team vertigo

Reflexive focus on operational objectives

Management team vertigo is an embarrassing discomfort, which often arises if *management team swell* is treated by rising too quickly to the top of a viewing tower. This syndrome is easy to explain with a down-to-earth metaphor. If a person is used to working on the ground, a rapid transition to the heights will easily cause a feeling of dizziness. That person will cling automatically to the nearest support. For a member of management team this means the following: If you are used to working on an operational basis, a rapid transition to strategic level will cause uncertainty, and so, at meetings, you quickly grab onto your own unitś operational issues. However, this emergency relief will only take you from bad to worse, namely because of operational focus you easily end up back at the painful *management team swell* again.

Care of management team vertigo

Management team vertigo is often very contagious, but, fortunately, the treatment of the disease is simple. *Management team vertigo* will pass quickly, when the management team together lets go of the operational handrail and focuses its attention on the goal on the horizon.

Image delusion

Pathetic complacency and omnipotent hallucinations

Image delusion is a disease of numerous management team members. For such a patient membership of a management team has become an end in itself. The disease leads to taking action on the safe side and to distortion of focus. This in turn leads to the primary pursuit of retaining oneś own position in the management team, for as long as possible. *Image delusion* makes the patient feel a certain satisfaction, and before long, pathetic complacency begins to shine on the face of the patient.

Image delusion care

There is no actual treatment for *image delusion* but many satisfied patients have reported about a miracle healing after receiving notice to quit from the management team.

At a team level, *image delusion* is associated with the contagious *navel hyperplasia*. This undermines the so-called business feel and critically reduces customer understanding in the management team. In the throes of this scourge the management team may even experience hallucinations of omnipotence. The team should be run down but it will be extremely difficult, thus, it will be better to wait for upcoming insolvency.

Secret society paralysis

Eyes turn inwards, environment suffers from information hunger

Secret society paralysis is a very typical disease in management teams. The disease is hardly noticeable within the team, but it silences all communications going out from the team. The management team becomes incapable of looking at the outside world and communicating its decisions. The team members turn their focus inward, and care only that each has the required information on issues for discussion and decision-making. *Secret society paralysis* culminates in mouths being firmly closed when the team members come out of the meeting. In the background to this disease there can be a childlike ego-centrism and a distorted perception of information hunger within the working community.

Care for secret society paralysis

Secret society paralysis can be treated with a stick or a carrot. An uncomfortable and also precarious treatment is the development of hunger awareness through a long lasting information fast. A more comfortable way is to make a strict management team decision, distribute even a very small amount of information, and then to focus strong-mindedly outwards, observing the positive reactions that the crumbs of information cause. After that the size of an information portion should be increased gradually, until communication becomes a natural part of the functioning of a healthy management team.

Meeting syndrome

Working alone, frustration and lack of inspiration

The risk of *meeting syndrome* is very notable in every management team. The disease takes two extreme forms. In the more common form the management team meets so often that the attention of the members is all the time on preparations for the upcoming meeting. This means mostly planning and fine-tuning of one's own presentation. Once the meeting is over one has to start preparation for the next meeting. *Meeting syndrome* does not add to a sense of community as the thorough preparation needs to be done alone and this of course reduces possibilities for discussion.

The second form of *meeting syndrome* is known by the name *hyper agenda syndrome* and it appears at infrequently held meetings. The agendas of those meetings are always long as your arm and clueless as regards logic. Decisions are often made before the meeting, which therefore only acts as a rubberstamp. Meeting syndrome makes management team members lose the meaning of their actions, and enthusiasm evaporates. The most horrifying threat is severe frustration and an irresistible desire to get away.

Care of meeting syndrome

A recommended treatment is magic spell care: collect greetings from sensible people and repeat these greetings regularly in the management team meetings, until the meeting syndrome disappears. A typical magic spell can be as follows: „Dad/Mom, why do you play the meeting game if you canĤ talk with your friends?‰ Unfortunately, magic spell care does not work on meeting-zombies, because the disease has eaten their souls.

An alternative form of care for *meeting syndrome* is a radical reform of meeting structures and injecting energy into meeting situations. The energy exhumation process requires risk-taking. It means taking interest in the sources of inspiration and energy wells of team members. When the energy is released into the system, healing will commence.

Goal itch, malignant leadership, human blindness

Blurred sense of reality, even blindness

Goal itch is roughly an opposite phenomenon to that earlier described as *management team vertigo*. High in a panoramic location it is easy to direct your focus onto a goal far away. At the same time, attention is drawn to the fact that, seen from a high position, the progress down there seems annoyingly slow. This is similar to standing in an observation tower and reviewing the progress of the work only from a distance. There you can see the whole picture, but at the same time, you wait more and more impatiently for the slow changes in the big picture.

Goal itch weakens the ability in the management team to see human beings and their activities that take them towards the goal. Bad *goal itch* causes a blurred sense of reality and cold behaviour toward subordinates. These commonly lead to a diagnosis of *malignant leadership* that may develop into *human blindness*. Chronic goal itch is always dangerous for collaboration and long-term success.

Goal itch care

The recommended treatment for all levels of goal itch is plenty of exercise on the ground around the ivory tower, with eyes open, ears open, stopping regularly. At the same time you stir up courage to question all existing goals and to update them with insights learned from the system. When a management team has achieved the ability to change their goals dynamically, this shows it has been healed from *goal itch*.

Culture abscess

Odour nuisances and blaming

Culture abscess is not actually a management team disease, but the management team is often the source of the disease and its most powerful transmitter. In a management team that is polluted by culture abscess, you hear often the argument: the management team would create success, but we have this kind of culture and that kind of people. Many of the organization researchers have the opinion that everything drains downwards in an organization. Therefore, the management affects the culture more than employees. At worst, it is not even appropriate to talk about the *draining culture abscess*, which means the organization is blessed with „long live the sacred cows%culture.

A remarkable diagnosis creator and leadership professional, Arto Hiltunen, has said the management in Finland has learned to live with its problems. Hiltunen means that companies continue despite the problems – and without solving the problems! In Hiltunen̂s opinion a typical management team is like a County Council: the delegates have designated places, where they sit holding noses high. The real decisions are made elsewhere – and the same is true also of many top-level management teams. According to legislation and corporate by-laws, in most cases, a body called management team simply does not exist. Regardless of where the management team is in the organization chart, it can be said that, in practice, nearly every management team leader could make all the decisions alone. And that even happens very often, which is one of the primary reasons of *culture abscess*. So the pus drains.

Care of culture abscess

The best treatment for *culture abscess* is an intense regimen of looking in the mirror. It can be forced, after every meal at least once every two hours, by taking a cleaning dose of wondering „what kind of culture is needed here – and what will that mean for the activities of the management team%The cleansing treatment starts with the management team and the results are then allowed to drain downwards.

Sacred cow disease

Avoidance to broach issues and silent sprouting of culture abscesses

Sacred cow disease has its breeding ground in a management team whose greatest strength is that it has learned to live with its problems. This team is a kind of group of naked emperors, who have learned not to talk about their embarrassing lack of clothing. This type of conscious living in a common lie will have an effect at an unconscious level by paralysing trust and degenerating commitment. In the case of this disease, it is good to recall its cultural ties. It is well known that the cow is a sacred animal in India and it is treated as it deserves. Cows are allowed to pass and lie down anywhere, and it really seems that Indians do not even see them. The invisible things within a management team with *sacred cow disease* are visible to everybody else but the disease lulls us into believing that those things are not supposed to be seen. It is easy to come up with a list of sacred cows: abuse, lying, injustice, under-achievement, alcoholism, breach of promise, incompetence, inadequate qualification, etc.

Care of sacred cow disease

A proven treatment for *sacred cow disease* is to talk about everything that is perceivable. Jack Welch from General Electric had a great piece of advice: Tell people the truth, because they know the truth anyway. The disease will vanish when you create word by word and issue by issue a new culture which provides the freedom to speak about everything.

It should be noted here that the name of the disease derives from India, but also there many people even say that cows impede traffic and city life. Therefore, Indiâs larger cities have special cowcatchers who take cows to the government-approved cow sanctuaries on the outskirts of the city. The cowcatchers come from lower castes and they are poorly paid civil servants, and every religious Hindu despises them. People interfere with their work even by stoning them. But this is a risk that is hardly likely to materialize in any management team.

Power scabies

Extremes of behaviour and an infected atmosphere

Power scabies is a very annoying disease in management teams at all levels. The occurrence of the disease always has very negative effects on confidence. *Power scabies* is identified by the behaviour of individual members of management teams. Specific features of the disease include the following:

- The need to be honoured and to be treated in an exceptional way. The affected individuals do not wait for their turn, they desire to obtain extra perks and want to be first. They also demand undivided attention. If their wish is neglected, they will be annoyed and irritated – even enraged.
- Glorification or annulment. The patients so affected either immediately idolize or invalidate their discussion partner. They flatter, adore, admire and praise or instead, frown on, offend and humiliate the other. There are no forms of behaviour in between.
- The emphasis is on self. The power scabies patient boasts continually. The speech repeats me, myself, and I. At the same time the disease removes the ability to take an interest in others and their words. His or her behaviour tends towards the bored and ignorant, if the patient is not the centre of the discussion.

- An inability to empathise. The most obvious sign of power scabies is the lack of ability to accommodate the other personŝ position. Patients are constantly stuck in their own little world and they seek to justify their own experience and their being right – in one way or another.

Power scabies care

Power scabies occurs at many levels. Patients do not recognize their illness, but at worst, this illness will inflame the atmosphere in the entire management team. Early diagnosis and the protection of the rest of the team are important. If the disease is deep-rooted in the leader of the management team, the team can provide feedback on their observations, directly to the patient, as well as to his or her manager. The only remedy is assertive action and a clear tackling of the non-permitted behaviour.

Unfortunately, the disease only loses strength when the carrier of the disease comes up against the wall a sufficient number of times, and learns humility. But sheer servility and bootlicking is not enough. An extreme form of care is compulsory treatment, in which the patient is completely isolated from the rest of the community.

Diversity indigestion, condensation of collective irrationality

Heartburn, name-calling, condensed stupidity

Diversity indigestion is very common in all management cultures on this planet. From mildly annoying heartburn and name-calling behind the back, its symptoms range to the worst verbal abuse and even physical aggression. Progressing to *divergence catarrh*, the disease results in team formation only from similar personalities, which is often followed by harmful *condensation of collective irrationality*. Outside the management team it is called more prosaically *group stupidity*.

As an internal management team disorder *diversity indigestion* is very tedious. In particular, within team members, the symptoms seem to begin with differences of temperament or opinion, but the real reason lies in motherŝ milk.

Care of diversity indigestion

Diversity indigestion is a treatable management team disease. The disorder is treated (forcibly or voluntarily) by injections of a gradually strengthening dose of different ways of thinking and operating styles. In this desensitization care a diversity germ, which causes the symptoms, is inserted on a regular basis into the mind and body of the carrier. The treatment requires patience, because the immune tolerance has several levels, and if indigestion symptoms reappear, the medication must always be adjusted down to the previous dose level. Studies have shown that visits to „diversity places‰of the patientŝ own-initiative will expedite the healing process. The levels of desensitization care together with their expected effects are described below.

Dosing Size 1: Approach

First select a sufficiently different „other%d(note: not yet the most disruptive „other%d) and practise in front of a mirror the question: „What is the positive aim of your actions?%dAfter the question becomes routine, it is time to test the power of the question in a real situation. It is important to protect yourself during this encounter. The best way to do it is to write down the substantial parts of the replies of the „others%dwhile listening. After this has been repeated with 3–5 different „others%dwithout symptoms, it is time to move on to the next dose size.

Dosing Size 2: Observe and explore

On the second level attention is directed towards occurrence of symptoms for a period of 1–2 weeks. The patient has a diary, in which he records all of the situations where the symptoms occur. When the test period has ended, the diary entries are carefully analysed. If you have succeeded in overcoming all the symptoms in the company of your colleagues during the monitoring process, you will be ready for the next level.

Dosing Size 3: Encounter

On the third level desensitization is already well advanced. The foundation has now been built up for several weeks and it is time to let the patient come to an extended encounter with a different „other%din the real world. Over an agreed period you undertake, with a different „other%da joint project, which will generate very high desensitization levels. When the process is finished, go through the experience with the following key questions.

- How was the diversity of the „other%of benefit to the project?
- How did you manage to bring out the strengths of your diversity?
- In which situations did the symptoms of diversity indigestion still occur?
- How did you manage to keep your reactions under control?
- What would you do differently now, in order to ensure an even better outcome?

After having accomplished several similar projects without symptoms the disease will have been defeated to a large extent.

Dosing Size 4: Praise and give thanks

The final confirmation of curbing the disease is the fact that the disease carrier is capable of giving positive feedback to different „others%din everyday situations.

When positive feedback comes genuinely and spontaneously, without any symptoms, desensitization has done its job. *Diversity indigestion* will usually be emphasized under stressful conditions, but there is a first-aid technique, which is recommended, that connects all management team members to an early emotional stage, in which *diversity indigestion* has not yet appeared, i.e. to the mother–child relationship. Thus, serve them with milk in identical mugs or bottles. Although the stubborn ones will not be healed with this, others will have more fun in continuing the meeting.

Silo inflammation

Isolation, avoidance of collaboration, solo playing

Silo inflammation is a well-known disease in many management teams. Silo inflammation is best recognized by the fact that between meetings the members of the management team potter around in their own silos and focus on issues concerning their own teams. The inflammation causes interest in dealing with colleagues to vanish. Also, common issues in the management team look distant. *Silo inflammation* spreads very easily and if left untreated it will infect the entire organization by causing people to isolate themselves in their silos, avoiding distracting initiatives to cooperate with other departments or business units. In the management team *silo inflammation* manifests itself in the duration of focus on action for the common good, which scarcely lasts the time of a standard meeting. Infected patients can put up with the others in the same room for only a few hours a month. In between the meetings the inflammation will surely keep the members apart.

Silo inflammation care

The recommended treatment for this disease is a radical compulsory care given by senior management. Patients are forced to give feedback concerning things outside their silos, and at the same time they are exposed to feedback from others. This is repeated, increasing the amount of feedback, until the usefulness of the feedback and cooperation will begin to develop an antibody to silo inflammation. The treatment can be boosted by low monetary doses of and special treatments, which are administered to the patient immediately after an obvious crossing of silo boundaries.

Positivity intolerance, yummy-yummy allergy, fault eye

Discouraging negativity and tragicomic pursuit of truth

Positivity intolerance is a general phenomenon in many Nordic cultures, but in the toughest management teams it has developed into so called *yummy-yummy allergy*. Even a minuscule portion of praise or positivity causes pimples to an allergic person. The starting point for this disease is a morbid pursuit of realism.

In the background there is often an underlying tendency towards perfectionism and being straightforward, which are called honesty by the patient.

A *yummy-yummy* allergic management team generally sets the goals high. If the goal is not achieved, the result is unambiguously „poor‰ and the members don't even try to say anything positive about it. If the goal is reached or even exceeded, they state: the result is in line with the goal. Strongly influenced by alcohol, someone may slip in a hyper exaggerating expression „not bad‰ but the state will very soon change to honest hangover.

Positivity intolerance often develops an additional discomfort, so-called *fault eye*. The patient finds faults and mistakes all the time and everywhere. The patient may be secretly even proud of this ability to find quality defects (but not too proud). The worst pain for a patient with positivity intolerance is praise without reason – and the only reasonable praise are comments like „the deceased was a good man in life‰ This kind of communication discourages and saddens a normal, living human being. *Yummy-yummy allergic* people put dampers on the enthusiasm and productivity of the healthy.

Positivity intolerance care

While planning the care of *positivity intolerance*, it is important to note the undisputed research findings of background variables with this disease. Patients totally miss information stemming from undeniable evidence derived from positive psychology, according to which positive things are worth taking into account. They also lack the knowledge obtained from brain research that positively records the first step towards the goal stimulates problem-solving skills in the brain. It is also typical that sadly they also lack a place in the brain to receive such information.

Anyone can heal negative brain, but it has to be done gently and patiently. Actual observations of small successes without overstatements, whilst at the same time observing the reactions of the patient, will help the brain to experience a light satisfaction. This will gradually create space for the insight that realism, great honesty and perfectionism also may include small successes, which affect the mood, and one day this brain will produce the first positive reaction: „Good – with all its shortcomings‰

Management team oedema

Stiffness in decision-making and dreariness of interaction

Management team oedema (swelling) is a rather common disease. It has its roots in thoughtlessness and sheer goodness, which lead to a tendency to form the widest possible group of decision makers, representing all the different parts of the organization. The *swelling* is very easy to diagnose – like counting the fingers on one hand. Namely, the initial symptoms appear when the management team has more than seven members. If the group size goes over ten, *management team oedema* becomes a serious problem. Activities slow down, decision-making becomes stiff and going through the agenda only makes a scratch on the surface.

Management team oedema care

The prevention and treatment for this disease is realism. For example, when evaluating the structure of the team, it is good to remember that decision-making and communicating decisions are two different things. The risk of *management team oedema* is significantly reduced if you manage to root out *secret society paralysis*, which effects communication and interaction. *Swelling* does not occur when the team size is seven or fewer.

When planning the treatment, it is important to remember that the management team does not need to be based on the existing organizational structure. Particularly, when the emphasis is on low organization, *swelling* tends to be strong. To block the swelling tendency, it is also good to remember the mathematical laws related to the size of the team. The number of interaction relations in the team grows after a certain point into uncontrollable dimensions. If you look first at bilateral relations, then the individual relationships are as follows:

    2 members: 2 relations
    3 members: 6 relations
    4 members: 12 relations
    5 members: 20 relations
    6 members: 30 relations
    7 members: 42 relations
    8 members: 54 relations
    9 members: 72 relations
    10 members: 90 relations

When we add into the calculation the various combinations of three, four, etc., the number of different variations multiplies. If we then look at the figures through the eyes of a statistical mathematician, we will encounter permutation, which is the act of arranging all the members of a set into some sequence or order. The number of interaction lines in a management team multiplies, when you look at ways of how to put people of a team in a different order. Then we use the concept of factorial (marked with an exclamation mark!) in our calculation, and various orders in the team are generated as follows:

    2 members: 2! i.e. 2×1 = 2 (A speaks first and then B or first B speaks and then A)
    3 members: 3! 3×2×1 = 6
    4 members: 4×3×2×1 = 24
    5 members: 5×4×3×2×1 = 120
    6 members: 6×5×4×3×2×1 = 720

    7 members: $7 \times 6 \times 5 \times 4 \times 3 \times 2 \times 1 = 5{,}040$
    8 members: $8 \times 7 \times 6 \times 5 \times 4 \times 3 \times 2 \times 1 = 40{,}320$
    9 members: $9 \times 8 \times 7 \times 6 \times 5 \times 4 \times 3 \times 2 \times 1 = 362{,}880$
    10 members: $10 \times 9 \times 8 \times 7 \times 6 \times 5 \times 4 \times 3 \times 2 \times 1 = 3{,}628{,}800$

Management team oedema blocks the interaction channels, so the controllable amount of interaction relationships in a Stellar Team is between 5–7 persons.

Boss constipation

Senselessness of a sensible director

Boss constipation is a disease of a management team leader, and it is very interesting because the team suffers more from it than the patient. When a management team leader knows everything and manages everything best, his or her pain starts when choosing members for the team. All the others are so much on a lower level in everything that the director begins to develop a sense of personal strength. If the strength develops so aggressively that it even begins to radiate around him or her, it becomes *boss constipation*. In the organization the ailment can often be heard in the form of the quiet expression „we have a strong leader‰

What about the patient? He or she feels that his or her stakeholders are not entirely neutral with respect to his or her decisions. Here the boss has a balance to find between openness and inclusion. He or she knows that good leadership should take into account different views and ideas of the parties; this should even include listening to dissenting views. He or she knows that the things that are needed to support decision-making should be tested and reflected on together with the right people. But, what when there are no right people . . .? The patient will have to withdraw and decide everything alone.

Care of boss constipation

A coaching course is recommended as treatment for *boss constipation*, where the patient will learn how to ask and to listen. The result is the insight that he/she can have a dialogue with the „weak ones‰ without contaminating or diluting „strong‰ leadership with weaker thoughts. Gradually, the body starts to produce a natural laxative to *boss constipation*, confidence, and a growing number of issues can be taken into discussion. As a by-product, weaker people receive space in which to grow and become stronger. Just by the simple act of the leader genuinely listening to them.

Note for the members of a „weak management team‰ the *boss constipation* patient is lonely, and the disease is associated, above all, with his or her own emotions, feelings and pressures. A lack of confidence often excludes the private side of life, and patients are not able to speak of their own disappointments, negative emotions, excitement or happiness. In their director-position patients regard the expression of matters related to emotions as a sign of weakness.

However, humanity can support the leadership. It is a drug that relieves *boss constipation* and changes the management culture and management team culture little by little. It will take a lot of courage to genuinely expose your humanity. It requires a whole new range of language patterns from the management team to be able to communicate the ability to perceive the emotional world of others. This also provides a new commitment to collaboration. Humanity is a good medicine also because it will not rule out the abilities of decision-making and performing profitable action. To test this you can try out, for example, the method „10-minute success-oriented coaching‰in Chapter 15.

Change motion sickness

Inappropriate action

Change motion sickness is a relatively normal affliction for many of us. It is also often described as „feeling sick‰In practice, the feeling is caused in a change journey by the bends that arrive as a disruption for our brains expecting to advance in rectilinear motion. The sickness goes away relatively soon, and depending on the bends of change, the recovery takes perhaps only a few seconds – or in the case of sensitive individuals, a few months.

Even though the disease is well known, its appearance in the management team worries the entire organization. Inappropriate action is then detected in the management team. Basically, it is presumed that the management team has planned the change journey and its road map so precisely that not a single bend will come as a surprise. However, hardly any level of planning in advance can prevent *change motion sickness* totally, even within the management team. Surprises will always come.

Care of change motion sickness

A recommended relief is resilience coaching, which strengthens the characteristics that make the sick feeling pass quickly, and then performance recovers to an appropriate level both for the individual and the team.

Resource blindness and advice deafness

Fading faith in resources or delusion of managing well

Resource blindness is in most management team cases blind faith in oneŝ own resources. The first symptom is fairly elevated optimism, so the team often sets goals that are over optimistic and beyond their possibilities. The management does not understand its own resources defect in proportion to the complexity of the objective. *Resource blindness* can also prevent the team from seeing how resources are misallocated and sometimes results in even a realistic goal not being achieved. Without proper treatment the consequences are fatal, for example, a fairly healthy business may be given over to cheap amputation.

A second variation of *resource blindness* is caused by too low optimism. This form is rare in management teams but at an individual level it is classified „almost as a public health problem%in some northern cultures. It blurs faith in one͡s own resources and causes the secondary symptom of impaired distance assessment capability. These patients set their goals too unambitiously with respect to their resources.

Resource blindness care

Management team resource blindness can be healed only when we administer the strongest possible form of treatment. This takes the form of eye-opening, profound coaching with a qualified team coach. A strong team process will improve abilities to see opportunities, judgement and performance – almost without exception – rising above the pre-sickness level. *Resource blindness* is closely related to *advice deafness*. Both diseases cause an illusion of the ability to cope alone. Despite this illusion, many *advice deaf* patients turn to a coach, as in coaching they will be allowed to suggest their own advice. The disease will be healed most certainly, as soon as the patient sets the healing itself as his or her goal.

References and sources

Aarnikoivu, H. 2010. *Aidosti hyödyllinen kehityskeskustelu*. 1st edition. Helsinki: Kauppakamarikustannus.

Alahuhta, M. 2013. Näin syntyy Koneen henki, Interview. Talouselämä. 7/12. Helsinki.

Argyris, C., Schön, D. 1978. *Organizational Learning: A Theory of Action Perspective*. 1st edition. Boston: Addison-Wesley Publishing Company.

Bandura, A. 1997. *Self-efficacy: The Exercise of Control*. 1st edition. London: Worth Publishers.

Bargh, J.A. 2011. „Unconscious Thought Theory and its Discontents: A Critique of the Critiques‰*Social Cognition*, 29(6), 629–647.

Bergqvist, J.T. 2007. *Superproductivity: The Future of Finland*. Espoo: Aalto University.

Brinol, P., Petty, R.E. 2003. „Overt Head Movements and Persuasion: A Self-validation Analysis‰*Journal of Personality and Social Psychology*, 84, 1123–1139.

Brown, R. 1988. *Group Processes: Dynamics within and between Groups*. 1st edition. Oxford: Blackwell Publishers.

Ciulla, J.B. 2004. *Ethics, the Heart of Leadership*. 2nd edition. Westport: Praeger Publishers.

Clutterbuck, D. 2009. *Coaching the Team at Work*. 1st edition. London: Nicholas Brealey International.

Clutterbuck, D. 2013. *Creating a Coaching Leadership Culture*. Keynote speech. Helsinki. October 18, 2013.

Clutterbuck, D., Megginson, D. 2005. *Making Coaching Work: Creating a Coaching Culture*. 1st edition. London: Chartered Institute of Personnel & Development.

Clutterbuck, D., Megginsson, D. (eds) 2013. *Beyond Goals: Effective Strategies for Coaching and Mentoring*. New York: Routledge.

Collins, J., Porras, J.I. 1994. *Built to Last: Successful Habits of Visionary Companies*. New York: Harper Business Essentials.

Conner, D. 1992. *Managing at the Speed of Change*. 1st edition. New York: Random House.

Conner, D. July 15, 2013. *The Real Story of the Burning Platform*. www.connerpartners. com/frameworks-and-processes/the-real-story-of-the-burning-platform August 15, 2012. Blogpost.

Conner, D., Hoopes, L. 2004. *Managing Change with Personal Resilience: 21 Keys for Bouncing Back & Staying on Top in Turbulent Organizations*. Raleigh, NC: MK Books.

Cooperrider, D.L., Srivastva, S. 1987. „Appreciative Inquiry in Organizational Life‰ *Research in Organizational Change and Development*, 1, 129–169.

Covey, S.M.R. 2006. *The SPEED of Trust: The One Thing that Changes Everything*. 1st edition. New York: Free Press.

De Dreu, Weingart, L.R. 2003. „Task Versus Relationship Conflict, Team Performance, and Team Member Satisfaction: A Meta-Analysis‰*Journal of Applied Psychology*, 88.4, 741–749.

Dobelli, R. 2012. *Selkeän ajattelun taito*. 1st edition. Helsinki: HS-kirjat.

Dobelli, R. 2013. *The Art of Thinking Clearly*. London: Sceptre.

Drucker, P.F. 1967. *The Effective Executive*. 1st edition. New York: Harper & Row.

Elliot, C. 1999. *Locating the Energy for Change: An Introduction to Appreciative Inquiry*. 1st edition. Winnipeg: International Institute for Sustainable Development.

Fairhurst, G.T., Grant, D. 2010. „The Social Construction of Leadership: A Sailing Guide‰ *Management Communication Quarterly*, 24(2), 171–210.

Fischer, M. 2012. *Linkages between Employee and Customer Perceptions in Business-to-business Services – Towards Positively Deviant Performances*. (Doctoral Dissertation). Helsinki: Aalto University.

Fredrickson, B.L., Branigan, C. 2005. „Positive Emotions Broaden the Scope of Attention and Thought–Action Repertoires‰*Cognition and Emotion*, 19, 313–332.

Fredrickson, B.L., Losada, M.F. 2005. „Positive Affect and the Complex Dynamics of Human Flourishing‰*American Psychologist*, 60(7), 678–686.

Gilbert, D. 2005. *Stumbling on Happiness*. 1st edition. New York: Vintage Books.

Goldsmith, M., Lyons, L., Freas, A., Witherspoon, R. 2000. *Coaching for Leadership: How the Worldß Greatest Coaches Help Leaders Learn*. 1st edition. New York: Jossey-Bass.

Goleman, D. 1996. *Emotional Intelligence*. 10th edition. New York: Bantam Dell, 2006.

Grant, A.M. 2007. „When Own Goals Are a Winner‰*Coaching at Work*, 2(2), 32–35.

Hackman, J.R. 2002. *Leading Teams: Setting the Stage for Great Performances*. 1st edition. Boston: Harvard Business School Press.

Hämäläinen, R.P., Saarinen, E. (eds) *Systeemiäly 2005*. Helsinki University of Technology.

Hawkins, P. 2011. *Leadership Team Coaching: Developing Collective Transformational Leadership*. 1st edition. London: Kogan Page.

Heinonen, S., Klingberg, R., Pentti, P. 2012. *Kaikkien aivot käyttöön*. 1st edition. Helsinki: SanomaPro.

Heron J. 1975. *Six-Category Intervention Analysis*. Human Potential Research Project, University of Surrey, Surrey, UK.

Hiltunen, A. 2012. *Johtamisen taito*. 1st edition. Helsinki: Sanoma Pro.

Hoopes, L., Mark, K. 2004. *Managing Change with Personal Resilience*. 1st edition. Raleigh: Mark Kelly Books.

Huczynski, A., Buchanan, D. 2010. *Organizational Behaviour: An Introductory Text*. 7th edition. 1st edition. New Jersey: Prentice-Hall.

Isen, A. M. 2000. „Positive Affect and Decision making‰In M. Lewis, J. Haviland-Jones (eds), *Handbook of Emotions*. 2nd edition, pp. 417–435. New York: Guilford.

Jungner, M. 2012. „Johtajat muutoksessa. Sankaruuden varjojen kohtaaminen‰Keynote speech. Espoo. August 24, 2012. Coaching Finland 2012.

Kahneman D. 2011. *Thinking, Fast and Slow*. 1st edition. New York: Macmillan.

Kahneman, D. 2012. *Ajattelu nopeasti ja hitaasti*. 1st edition. Helsinki: Terra Cognita.

Kahneman, D., Lovallo, D., Sibony, O. 2011. *The Big Idea: Before you Make that Big Decision*. 1st edition. Brighton: Harvard Business Review.

Katzenbach, J., Smith, D. 1993. *The Wisdom of Teams: Creating the High-performance Organization*. 1st edition. Boston: Harward Business School Press.

Keltner, D. 1995. „Signs of Appeasement: Evidence for the Distinct Displays of Embarrassment, Amusement, and Shame‰*Journal of Personality and Social Psychology*, 68(3), 441–454.

Keltner, D. 2009. *Born to Be Good: The Science of a Meaningful Life*. 1st edition. New York. W.W. Norton & Company.

Kirkman, B.L., Gibson, C.B., Shapiro, D.L. 2001. „ÆxportingÊTeams: Enhancing the Implementation and Effectiveness of Work Teams in Global Affiliates‰*Organizational Dynamics*, 30(1), 12–39.

Kotter, J.P. July 15, 2013. www.kotterinternational.com/our-principles/urgency 2011. Blogpost.

Kotter, J.P. 1996. *Leading Change*. Boston: Harvard Business School Press.

Kotter, J.P. 1996. *Muutos vaatii johtajuutta*. 1st edition. Helsinki: Rastor.

Kozlowski, S.W.J., Watola, D.J., Nowakowski, J.M., Kim, B.H., Isabel C.B. „Developing Adaptive Teams: A Theory of Dynamic Team Leadership‰In E. Salas, G. Goodwin, C.S. Burke (eds). *Team Effectiveness in Complex Organizations: Cross-disciplinary Perspectives and Approaches*, pp 113–155. New York: Routledge.

Ladkin, D. 2010. *Rethinking Leadership: A New Look at Old Leadership Questions*. 1st edition. Cheltenham: Edward Elgar Publishing.

LaFasto, F., Larson, C. 2001. *When Teams Work Best: 6000 Team Members and Leaders Tell what it Takes to Succeed*. 1st edition. Thousand Oaks, California: Sage.

Laine, N. 2008. *Trust in Superior–Subordinate Relationship*. Tampere: University of Tampere.

Laine P.-M., Meriläinen, S. 2013. *Ohjelmistoyritys epäjohtaa uudistumista*. Työn tuuli 1/2013. pp. 42 Helsinki: Henry ry.

Lencioni, P. 2002. *The Five Dysfunctions of a Team: A Leadership Fable*. 1st edition. San Francisco: Jossey-Bass.

Levitin, D.J. 2006. *This Is Your Brain on Music: The Science of a Human Obsession*. Dutton Adult.

Lipchik, E. 2012. *Emotion in Solution Focused Therapy*. Seminarium of Ratkes Association. May 9, 2012. Helsinki.

Losada, M., Heaphy, E. 2004. „The Role of Positivity and Connectivity in the Performance Business Teams: A Nonlinear Dynamics Model‰*American Behavioral Scientist*, 47(6), 740–765.

Luthans, F. 2013. *Positive Psychological Capital*. Lecture at Finlandia Hall. October 20, 2013. Helsinki.

Löytänä, J., Kortesuo, K. 2011. *Asiakaskokemus*. 1st edition. Helsinki: Talentum.

Manner, J. 2012. *Maailman paras johtoryhmä – 10 ratkaisevaa eroa*. 1st edition. Espoo. Memo.

Marion, R., Uhl-Bien, M. 2001. „Leadership in Complex Organizations‰*The Leadership Quarterly*, 12(4), 359–418.

Moreno, J.L. 1964. *Psychodrama*. Vol. 1. 1st edition. Beacon, New York: Beacon House.

Moreno, J.L. 1977. *Psychodrama*, Vol. 1. 5th edition. Beacon, New York: Beacon House.

Nadler, R. 2009. *What Was I Thinking? Handling the Hijack*. www.psychologytoday.com

Naquin, C.E., Tynan, R.O. 2003. „The Team Halo Effect: Why Teams are not Blamed for their Failures‰*Journal of Applied Psychology*, 88, 332–340.

Neill, J. 2006. *What is Psychological Resilience?* www.wilderdom.com

Oikarinen, T. 2008. *Organisatorinen oppiminen. Tapaustutkimus oppimisprosessin jännitteistä teollisuusyrityksessä. Acta Universitatis Lappeenrantaensis 299*, Dissertation. University of Technology, Lappeenranta. Digipaino.

Olson, B.J., Parayitam, S., Yongijan, B.Y. 2007. „Strategic Decision Making: The Effects of Cognitive Diversity, Conflict, and Trust on Decision Outcomes‰*Journal of Management*, 33.2, 196–222.

212   References and sources

Ordóñez, L.D., Schweitzer, M.E., Galinsky, A.E., Bazerman, M.H. 2009. „Goals Gone Wild: The Systematic Side Effects of Overprescribing Goal Setting‰*Academy of Management Perspectives*, 23(1), 6–16.

Paananen, I. 2013. „Start-up Philosophy‰ Speech at Talouselämä 500 Seminarium, Helsinki.

Parppei, R. 2008. *Business Coaching as a Development Intervention of Self-Regulation*. Dissertation. Helsinki University of Technology.

Peters, T., Waterman, R.H. 1982. *In Search of Excellence: Lessons from America's Best-Run Companies*. New York: Harper & Row.

Reina, D.S., Reina, M.L. 2006. *Trust and Betrayal in the Work-place: Building Effective Relationships in your Organization*. 1st edition. San Francisco: Berrett-Koehler Publishers.

Ribb, S., Kourdi, J. 2004. *Trust Matters: For Organisational and Personal Success*. 1st edition. New York: Palgrave Macmillan.

Rinne, T. 2009. *Myrskyn jälkeen – johtamisen ja coachingin parhaita käytäntöjä talousmyrskystä selviytymisen arkeen*. 1st edition. Helsinki: Tammi.

Rispens, S., Greer, L., Jehn, K.A. 2007. „It could be worse: A study on the alleviating roles of trust and connectedness in intragroup conflicts‰ *International Journal of Conflict Management*, 18.4, 325–344.

Ristikangas, M.-R., Ristikangas, V. 2010. *Valmentava johtajuus*. 1st edition. Helsinki: WSOYpro.

Ristikangas, V., Aaltonen, T., Pitkänen, E. 2008. *Asiantuntijasta esimies. Arvostusta ja innostusta esimiestyöhön*. 1st edition. Helsinki: WSOYpro.

Ristikangas, V., Junkkari, L. 2011. *Sukset ristissä. Omistajien, hallituksen ja johdon yhteistyö*. 1st edition. Helsinki: Kauppakamarikustannus.

Rubin, I.M., Plovnick, M.S., Fry, R.E. 1977. *Task Oriented Team Development*. 1st edition. New York: McGraw-Hill.

Ryan, R., Deci, E., Niemiec, C. 2009. „The Path Taken: Consequences of Attaining Intrinsic and Extrinsic Aspirations in Post-college Life‰*Journal of Research in Personality*, 73(3), 291–306.

Saarikallio, S. 2010. „Musiikin tunne-elämykset arkielämässä‰In J. Louhivuori, S. Saarikallio (eds), *Musiikkipsykologia*. Jyväskylä: Atena.

Saarinen, E. 2013. *Filosofia ja systeemiajattelu*. Lecture series. Aalto University Espoo.

Saarinen, E., Hämäläinen, R. 2004. „Systems Intelligence: Connecting Engineering Thinking with Human Sensitivity‰In Raimo P. Hämäläinen and Esa Saarinen (eds), *Systems Intelligence – Discovering a Hidden Competence in Human Action and Organizational Life*, Helsinki University of Technology: Systems Analysis Laboratory Research Reports, A88, October.

Saarinen, E., Hämäläinen, R., Martela, M., Luoma, J. 2008. *Systems Intelligence Thinking as Engineering Philosophy*. Helsinki University of Technology.

Schein, E. 2004. *Organizational Culture and Leadership*. 1st edition. San Francisco: Jossey-Bass.

Schoorman, F.D., Mayer, R.C., Davis, J.H. 1995. „An Integrative Model of Organizational Trust‰*Academy of Management Review*, 20, 709–734.

Schwartz, B. 2004. *Paradox of Choice*. 1st edition. New York: Harper Perennial.

Seligman, M. 2011. *Flourish: A Visionary New Understanding of Happiness and Well-being*. 1st edition. New York: Simon and Schuster.

Silvan, S. 2006. *Valppaus on valttia*. 1st edition. Helsinki: Talentum.

Simons, D.J., Chabris, C.F. 1999. *Gorillas in our Midst: Sustained Inattentional Blindness for Dynamic Events*. 1st edition. Cambridge, MA: Harvard University Press.

Stanovich, K.E. 2012. *How to Think Straight About Psychology.* 10th edition. London: Pearson.

Swieringa, J., Wierdsma, A. 1992. *Becoming a Learning Organization: Beyond the Learning Curve.* 1st edition. Wokingham: Addison-Wesley.

Talouselämä 7/2013, „*Näin syntyy Koneen henki%*Interview of Matti Alahuhta.

Tensing, M., Kultalahti, L. 2010. *Ihmismielen toimintaa ymmärtävä strategia – Psykodynaaminen, systeeminen ja kokemuksellinen oppimisen teoria työhyvinvoinnin palveluksessa.* 1st edition. Oulu: Metanoia Instituutti.

Thornton, C. 2010. *Group and Team Coaching.* 1st edition. London: Routledge.

Uusitalo, T. et al. 2009. *Ennakoiva ja joustava turvallisuuden johtaminen. Resilienssi Suomessa.* Helsinki: VTT Research Report R-09394-09.

Wageman, R., Nunes, D., Burruss, J., Hackman, J.R. 2008. *Senior Leadership Teams: What it Takes to Make Them Great. Center for Public Leadership.* 1st edition. Brighton: Harvard Business Review Press.

Williams, A. 2002. Ryhmän salaisuudet. Sosiometria muutoksen voimavarana. Resurssi., WS Bookwell Oy, Juva. Translation of the original: 1991. *Forbidden Agendas: Strategic Action in Groups.* London: Routledge.

Woiceshyn, J. 2013. *Tulos ja moraali – eettinen tie menestykseen.* 1st edition. Helsinki: Kauppakamari.

Ylitalo, J. 2012. *Ohjauksellisen johtajuuskoulutuksen vaikuttavuuden rakentuminen.* Doctoral Dissertation 106/2012. Helsinki: Aalto University.

Zajonc, R. 2001. *Mere Exposure: A Gateway to the Subliminal.* 1st edition. California: Current Directions in Psychological Science, SAGE Publications.

Index

Entries in **bold** denote tables; entries in *italics* denote figures.